CHURCH
GROWTH
—— THROUGH THE ——
BUS
MINISTRY

CHURCH GROWTH
—THROUGH THE—
BUS
MINISTRY

Dr. Jeff Fugate

SWORD OF THE LORD
P U B L I S H E R S

Post Office Box 1099 • Murfreesboro, Tennessee 37133
(800) 247-9673 • (615) 893-6700
swordofthelord.com

All Scripture quotations are from
the King James Bible.

Printed and Bound in the United States of America

CONTENTS

III. The Principles of the Bus Ministry

IV. The Promotions and Visitation of the Bus Ministry

INTRODUCTION

M Y FATHER was a Baptist preacher. In July of 1972 when I was eight years old, he started the Bible Baptist Church in his hometown of Hazard, Kentucky. He started a bus ministry as soon as he started the church. That one route eventually grew to twelve routes in that little mountain county. At the early age of forty, Dad died, only thirteen years after having started the church. At the time of his death we were covering every road in our county and a few roads in surrounding counties with buses from our church.

I remember those old buses. The first three were forty-eight-passenger 1949 Chevrolet buses that had worn out long before we bought them. I remember two big International buses with no power steering and a bulldog first gear that you could outrun on foot. I can recall watching Dad work on those buses trying to make sure they were ready for the road on Sunday. Oh, the blessings we saw, and the miracles God performed in the bus ministry of that old country church!

My experience in the bus ministry began at the age of thirteen. At the age of sixteen, as soon as I was able to get my driver's license, I became a bus captain. I was just a teenager; but Dad took me to bus conferences, Sword Conferences and others, to hear men like Dr. Beebe, Dr. Rice, Dr. Hyles, Brother Roloff, and so many other great preachers of that day. In those meetings my heart was set on fire to do a work for God.

Now for over twenty-five years I have been a pastor building a church with a growing bus ministry. Writing about the bus ministry is second nature to me. It has been a part of my life for most of my life. I love to teach the methods of a ministry that is responsible for more people coming to Christ than any other ministry in our churches.

It is also exciting to know that the bus ministry is still going strong all over this country. While there have been hurdles and difficulties, it excites me to know that churches are still starting bus ministries, new routes are still being started, and new workers are surrendering to work in this great ministry.

Perhaps the most exciting thing is to meet people all over this nation who are products of the bus ministry. They are now adults who are faithful to church, win souls to Christ, tithe, live separated lives and have fine Christian homes. You may even be one of them, and now you are a part of reaching other children and families for Christ through the bus ministry.

In May of 1991, I became the pastor of the Clays Mill Road Baptist Church in Lexington, Kentucky. My first service was a Wednesday night with only eighteen people in attendance. Since then the Lord has allowed us to grow by an average of almost one hundred per year.

We now operate more than twenty bus routes with over a thousand riders each Sunday. More importantly, we are seeing people saved, baptized and taught the Word of God whom we never would have reached otherwise. Who works these routes? There are teenagers, adults, senior saints, businessmen, policemen, engineers, salesmen, housewives, mechanics, and people from almost every other walk of life. This army of workers give of their time, love and talents to reach young people for Christ.

You can't be around Jeff Fugate for very long without discovering that I love the bus ministry. It is not something I do because I am supposed to, or because everyone else is doing it, or because I feel I have to. I do it because I want to. I believe in it. I know we can have a greater impact for Christ in our city as long as we keep reaching young people and teaching them how to live for Christ.

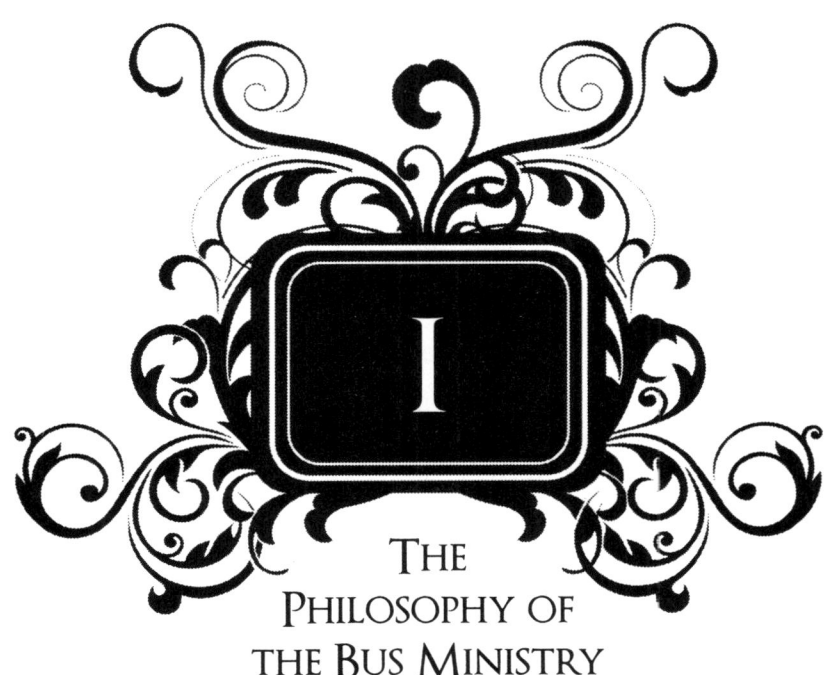

I

THE PHILOSOPHY OF THE BUS MINISTRY

My Burden for the Bus Ministry

THE BUS ministry has been a part of my life for over thirty years. I grew up in southeast Kentucky. My father was my pastor. Our church attendance grew to six hundred with more than four hundred riding in on the buses. In those days back in the seventies, we had Sunday school teachers, ushers and other workers who came to church on buses. Being brought up in the bus ministry was wonderful.

My father wore many hats back then. He was the pastor, the bus director, the bus mechanic, and everything else he needed to be in order to keep those buses on the road. I believe there were twelve bus routes in that country mountain church. I saw what a great tool it was for reaching people for Christ and what an effective way it was to serve the Lord in the local church. When my father died at the age of forty, I found myself taking his place at "the ripe old age" of twenty-one. That church was filled then and still is today with people who were reached through the bus ministry.

In 1991 the Lord moved me to Lexington, Kentucky, where I became pastor of Clays Mill Road Baptist Church. The time has certainly flown by, and God has continued to bless our church. One reason has been our commitment to the bus ministry.

In 2002 I became the editor of the *Church Bus News* which was founded by the late Wally Beebe—"Mr. Bus," as Dr. Hyles labeled him. Since then I have been conducting bus conferences all across America, including a national bus convention in Lexington. At the request of Dr. Shelton Smith, I am also writing a regular column in the *Sword of the Lord* on, of all things, the bus ministry.

By now you should be able to recognize the fact that I have a heart for the bus ministry. I love it. In fact, I believe it is more than a ministry, I believe it is the heart of the fundamental Baptist church. To me, it is not a "token ministry" but the greatest tool for fulfilling the Great Commission available to us today.

The bus ministry is a missionary work right here in America. While our wonderful foreign missionaries are called to leave home and country and serve on a foreign field, I see our bus captains and workers as missionaries reaching a part of a city or town that would not be reached without them.

As much as I love it, I have some concerns for the bus ministry in America. Because it is difficult work and because it is so costly to operate, I fear that it has often been pushed aside from where it once was in many churches. Far too often the bus ministry has become a "token ministry." We continue to do it, although often in a much reduced fashion, more because we feel we must rather than because we see its full purpose and potential.

Although I continue to believe that the bus ministry is the heart of fundamentalism, I fear that many have begun to work on the "image" of fundamentalism at the expense of a vibrant bus ministry. We seem more concerned with how we look or how we are accepted by others in the world and even in our own cities and towns, than in reaching more souls with this effective tool. In the past we were not ashamed of reaching the poor, the needy or the down-and-out with the Gospel.

Don't misunderstand me. I am not against having nice, first-class buildings and properties, but I am against giving up the greatest soul-winning tool fundamentalism has ever known in order to have these things.

In many churches we have started placing a greater emphasis on reaching the middle class. I am not against reaching the middle class. I am for it, and we all know that we must have money to care for the expenses and costs of the ministries of our church.

However, the Bible and the Lord Jesus NEVER emphasized reaching the middle class to the point of neglecting the poor. In fact, the Lord Jesus always emphasized reaching the poor. Our churches and Sunday schools should be organized in a manner where we reach and minister to every class of people, but it is not good nor right to neglect the poor of our cities and towns.

My heart's desire is to see a revival of this heart of fundamentalism, the bus ministry. I am working and praying for our churches to return to a recognition of and respect for this amazing ministry, praying that we will experience a revival of the bus ministry throughout this nation. A preacher once told me that I should be careful not to become known as the "bus man" instead of as a pastor. I told him and continue to declare that I am honored to be known as a pastor who loves and represents the bus ministry in America.

This book is designed to encourage pastors to get into or return to the bus ministry. Through these chapters I desire to help teach and equip pastors, bus directors and bus workers to build vibrant bus routes that will reach a great harvest of souls. My goal is to keep it practical and simple so that you could easily implement the ideas and principles into your work. In the words of one of my heroes, Dr. Wally Beebe, my goal in these pages is to **"keep those buses rolling."**

I'll Take the Bus Kids

ONE DAY Jesus was entertaining the little children. Can you picture Him with these irreverent little ones who were drawn to Him with childlike faith and enthusiasm? His disciples saw what was transpiring; and with a bit of indignation towards those who brought the little ones, the disciples tried to chase them away. After all, Jesus was a very important person, and they felt it was their duty to guard Him from the onslaught of those who might "waste" His time. Besides, you can't build the Kingdom (church) of God on kids. Jesus would have none of it, and I think I can almost hear Him say to those stuffy men, "I'll take the bus kids."

I know that is not exactly what He said, but it was akin to it in many ways. Look at what He did say:

"But when Jesus saw it, he was much displeased, and said unto them, Suffer the little children to come unto me, and forbid them not: for of such is the kingdom of God."—Mark 10:14.

I want you to take note of four things said here in this passage.

1. Jesus was displeased that the children were being kept away.
2. He told the disciples to do whatever it took to allow them to come to Him.
3. He commanded they not be told they could not come.

    4. He said that the kingdom of God is made of those like these children.

It is interesting to me that the greater a man's stature, the more those around him try to guard him from being bothered by "lesser" people such as children, poor people, sick people, hurting people, or broken people. Jesus was not willing to allow this to happen.

Perhaps that is why He went through Samaria without His disciples and without forewarning. The disciples may have attempted to chase away the woman at the well before Jesus arrived.

Many know the story of the phrase, "I'll take the bus kids." It is a story similar to the one we see in the Bible. Dr. Jack Hyles had taken the pastorate of a formalistic church of rather wealthy people. When he saw the lives of so many without Christ, he decided to go after the children through the bus ministry.

A few rich people in the church were tired of the inconveniences these children were bringing to "their" church, so they decided to confront Dr. Hyles with an ultimatum. Make no mistake about it, he loved these people equally. He wanted to be their pastor and to meet their needs, but they offered him an "either-or" proposition. They said, "Either you stop allowing those bus kids to be brought in, or we will leave. It's they or we."

In my heart I do not believe that Dr. Hyles pondered the question before speaking. When it comes to reaching the lost, one who has the mind of Christ does not have to think long before giving a response to such an ultimatum. In what would define his ministry forever, Dr. Hyles said, "I'll take the bus kids." The rest is history. He lost those rich people, and it grieved his heart to do so. However, he knew that it is people like the bus kids who make up the kingdom of Heaven, and they should never be forbidden from being brought to church.

Those bus kids now circle the globe preaching the Gospel and winning souls to Christ. More than ten years after Dr. Hyles' death, Mrs. Hyles said, "I get more letters and cards from bus kids who are still living for the Lord all over the world than from any other group of people."

Bus kids. Why is it that those words can carry such a stigma? It is because we think we know more about how Christ's church should be built than He does, just as the disciples thought they knew more about building the kingdom of Heaven than Jesus did. However, Jesus quickly and sternly put them in their place.

I believe that the bus ministry better represents what a New Testament church is all about than perhaps any other thing.

I hear all the excuses and accusations.

♦ You can't finance a church on bus kids.

♦ You will scare away people with money if you have a bunch of poor bus kids running around.

♦ You are just bribing them to come to have a bigger attendance.

Well, let me ask you these questions.

♦ How did Dr. Hyles leave the great First Baptist Church in Hammond, Indiana debt free with over 55 million dollars' worth in properties and cash in the bank if building with bus kids does not work?

♦ Why do we speak of the great Moody Church, built under the leadership of D. L. Moody, but forget that its great success came from his love of the young ruffians brought to church by none other than Mr. Moody himself?

♦ Finally, why is it all right to try to motivate children to do everything except come to church?

I am not trying to get Christian workers to choose any one group of people over another. Rather, I would like to get folks to place an emphasis on a ministry that is one of the greatest in reaching many lost souls for Christ. I want to instruct others on how to operate a bus ministry effectively and win as many people to Christ as possible. With that in mind, let me give you two important thoughts.

1. The bus ministry must be more than a "token ministry" in a Baptist church. It must not be merely a fulfillment of an obligation or to identify the church as being for the Great Commission. If our purpose is to preach the Gospel to every creature and to reach the poor and down-and-out and everyone else in our cities, towns and rural areas for Christ, why would we neglect the greatest tool we have for doing so? If I wanted a tool to drive a nail, why would I choose a screwdriver rather than a hammer? The bus ministry can be directed to large groups of people, and it is one ministry in which all aspects of the Great Commission can be fulfilled.

- ◆ Preaching the Gospel
- ◆ Getting new converts to church to be baptized
- ◆ Teaching them the Bible

Not using the bus ministry is like using a pole instead of a net to catch a lot of fish. I believe in casual soul winning just like I believe in casual fishing. Give me a pole on occasion, and I will catch me a fish. Give me a one-on-one opportunity to witness to someone, and I will lead a soul to Christ. However, if it is my job to catch fish, then give me the biggest net possible. In fact, give me several of them. The bus ministry is a net which allows us to do our job of reaching the lost most effectively.

2. The pastor needs to have the bus ministry in his own heart. Pastor, do not expect the bus ministry to be the passion of your people if it is not your passion. Men who try and fail to build a bus ministry do so most often because they wanted the results without the burden. They hoped their people would somehow "catch" the burden. It does not work that way. Jesus did not send out the disciples and hope they would "catch" the burden for the lost world.

- ◆ He pointed out the needy crowds.
- ◆ He taught them to care.
- ◆ He showed them how to reach people.
- ◆ He warned them of what to expect.

Jesus was the example, not merely the instructor. He did not organize the ministry and send them. He led them even as He organized the work. He was not a pusher; He was a leader. We must do the same; we must be the example to our people.

Pastor, if you really want to win the lost in your area in great numbers, sell out to the bus ministry. Do not assume that everybody belongs there. That is certainly not the case, but almost all Christian servants can find some role within the bus ministry. If not, help them find another place where they can win people to Christ.

Do not get up in your pulpit and scream, "I'll take the bus kids!" when no one is trying to stop you. Don't throw away an opportunity to win any group to Christ. However, let me make this one thing clear: If you really want to see the love of Christ in action, get neck-deep in this great ministry. It will bless your church and allow you truly to know the heart of our Saviour.

THE BENEFITS TO A CHURCH OF HAVING A BUS MINISTRY

SO, REALLY, what's the point? What is the bottom line as to why my church should have a bus ministry? I have heard arguments against it and stories of the problems churches have had because of their bus ministries. I have read of the law-suits and threats levied against churches with bus ministries. In fact, I have heard that the bus ministry is the cause of many thriving and growing churches' losing momentum and even going down to the point of being forced into bankruptcy. There have even been men who once had bus ministries who now bad-mouth them.

Have you had that conversation in your head? Has that opinion been a part of your thinking? There are many pastors who simply are afraid of starting a bus ministry because of the arguments they have heard against it.

- ◆ It is expensive.
- ◆ It can be a legal nightmare.
- ◆ The church can get out of balance.
- ◆ Bus kids can't financially support the church.
- ◆ You will drive away upper- and upper-middle-class people.
- ◆ The bus ministry destroyed the churches who were part of the great church growth movement of the '60s and '70s.
- ◆ It's just a numbers game.

Well, allow me to say that all of these arguments are partially true, but none of them is totally true.

◆ It is expensive unless you compare it to the number of souls saved per dollar spent.

◆ There have been a slight number of legal problems. Some have been caused by negligence, and some have not. All ministries have their risks, and one purpose of this book is to help churches reduce these risks.

◆ Churches can get out of balance, but most don't, and yours does not need to.

◆ Bus kids can't support the church, but God can bless financially the church that obeys His mandates.

◆ Any pastor who makes decisions based on who will stay or who will leave will not build a New Testament church. Some will leave, most will stay, and many will get involved. That is the bottom-line truth.

◆ Many things contributed to the decline of many of the churches that grew in the '60s and '70s, but the bus ministry was the least of those factors.

◆ Great emphasis is placed on numbers, but it is not a game to those of us who are attempting to proclaim the Gospel to the entire world. The more people, including children, to whom we give the Gospel, the more who will be saved.

Now let me tell you the other side of what the bus ministry does for a church. These are not things I have heard. These are things I have experienced personally first as a teenage bus worker and now as a veteran pastor and during all the years in between. When you compare the positives to the negatives, you will see what a great blessing the bus ministry can be to your church.

1. **Fulfilling the Great Commission.** How can any of us get away from the little phrases inserted within the commands of God's Word?

"...all the world..."

"...every creature..."

"...the highways and hedges..."

Those phrases are a big part of our mandate. We cannot—we must not—ignore them. The bus ministry is the greatest tool I have ever seen to accomplish these things. Show me a better one, and I will add it to my work, if it is scriptural.

2. **Obedience to go into the highways and hedges.** The church is to reach everybody, and that includes the ones who are on the outskirts of our world. My family and I live in a nice neighborhood. Honestly, there are places where I would not choose to live, and those places are where often there is no real gospel influence. We cannot ignore them, so how are we going to reach them? We can go soul winning there or conduct sidewalk Sunday schools, **but** the challenge is this: we are to add these people to the church. The best way to do that is to bus them in.

3. **Opportunities for people to serve.** Christian workers will not grow endlessly in their faith unless they are exercising their faith in service. The bus ministry is a place where many people can serve the Lord. Some of the most dedicated people I know are people who work in the bus ministry. Being a bus worker does something good for a person.

4. **Compassion for the poor.** God's Great Commission has far too often been replaced by the government's Great Society. The church thinks that conducting a food drive occasionally will mean they have obeyed the commands to reach and feed the poor. More poor people are fed by bus ministries than by any other ministry. Get to know a hungry and needy family and visit them every week, and you will develop a compassion you never had before. We don't speak often enough about the poor because we are only remotely aware of them. The bus ministry will make one personally aware of the poor.

5. **Expanding the outreach of the Gospel.** This is important because many churches are reaching their local areas and then foreign countries, but what of the inner cities of America? There is a mission field for you. Jesus went to heathen areas when He walked this earth. He preached in places that were hostile to the Gospel and in some cases even primitive culturally. He went beyond His local parish and reached out with a plan that would

later take the Gospel to the four corners of the world.

6. Loving the unloved. How many children go to bed every night without hearing anyone tell them they love them! Many have no father in the home, and Mom works twelve hours a day. Television is their main social influence. Tell one of these children that you love him, that God loves him, and watch his eyes brighten. It is amazing.

7. Energizing your people. For every "problem" the bus ministry brings, it brings hundreds of blessings. Sunday nights when we share with our people the blessings of the bus ministry, it energizes all of us to see what God has done in precious lives. Do you want to bring a new jolt of spiritual excitement into your church? Get into the work of the bus ministry, and see what God does to energize your people.

8. Seeing lives transformed. This is really the biggest reason for having a bus ministry and the reason that overcomes every objection. Missionaries come to our churches and tell of their work; but nothing does more to burden our hearts for their field than when they show pictures on a screen of individual people, while telling the miracle stories of what God has done in their lives. With a bus ministry, you won't need pictures. You can show those miracle stories live and in person. What a blessing that is!

Well, you may look at the reasons not to have a bus ministry, if you wish. As for me, I will accept the challenges that accompany having a bus ministry, because I know that the benefits **far** outweigh the difficulties. Yes, there is a right way and a wrong way to do it. That is true of everything. Read the rest of the pages of this book, and you will learn what to do and what not to do. Recognize the fact that for every one negative your church will encounter, there will be hundreds, yea, even thousands, of blessings.

WHAT'S IN IT FOR ME?
THE CHURCH MEMBERS
AND THE BUS MINISTRY

THE PASTOR has decided to take your church into the bus ministry or perhaps to expand upon one already in existence. You are a faithful and loyal member, and you want to know what you can do and what advantages it will bring to you and your church. Many people are excited about the new ministry, and others may be a bit reluctant or wary of it. You cannot help but wonder how this is going to affect you and your family. You have questions, but you do not want to appear negative by asking them.

In writing this book I felt there needed to be a chapter for good people who are members of churches getting into the bus ministry. Some of your concerns and questions are legitimate and ought to be addressed. Having been a pastor of a church with a vibrant bus ministry for more than twenty years helps me to understand your concerns and questions.

Let me begin by saying that you should not get involved in the bus ministry unless you believe God wants you to do so. It is not for everybody; and even if it is for you, perhaps now is not the time you should do it. Don't feel guilty and don't make excuses. If God is not in it and you are serving elsewhere, then be at peace about it. Don't feel pressured to join unless God is clearly leading you to do so. Otherwise, you will end up doing more harm to your spirit than good, and that will eventually affect others.

That said, there are three questions members often ask about the bus ministry.

1. What may I expect?
2. What are the benefits?
3. What can I do?

Hopefully these answers will help put your mind at ease and allow you to be one hundred percent supportive of the direction your church is taking.

What may I expect? There will be some noticeable changes that will take place when your church gets involved in a bus ministry. Here are a few.

♦ There will be more kids around; and with more kids, there will be more noise and messes. Kids are kids. They are full of energy and not always as courteous as they ought to be.

♦ There will be more buzz. With more kids come more energy and excitement. The hallways may get a little louder and a little more congested.

♦ There will be more people occupying the same space. This may sound silly, but let's face it: as hard as we may try to keep them out of your way, there may be a longer line in the restrooms or more congestion in the hallways.

♦ There will be more baptisms. I say this to prepare you that you may be a bit longer in the invitation and during the baptismal service, as many of these children will be accepting Christ as Saviour and getting baptized.

♦ There may be a bit more inconvenience leaving church. The buses may cause a need for detours in the route you normally take.

♦ There may be some misbehavior. Well, I didn't want to say it, but it is true. More kids mean more behavioral problems. Keep reminding yourself of when you were a kid.

♦ There will be financial responsibility. This will have an effect on your church budget. Buses cost money to operate; therefore, accept the fact that some of your tithes and offerings will be used for this new ministry.

◆ There will be some adjustments for everybody. The best leader learns as he goes. The pastor will anticipate what is best only to discover that his plans did not work; then changes will have to be made. Please be patient as things get started.

What are the benefits? Did I discourage you? Well, let me tell you about the benefits of the bus ministry, and hopefully it will help you realize that it is well worth all the challenges associated with it.

◆ Precious souls will be saved. Many will be children. Think of it. You will be reaching them before they have gotten old and cold to the Gospel.

◆ Lives will be transformed. Children will ride your bus and grow to be fine Christians because your church cared to reach them and teach them.

◆ There will be more energy. I mentioned that in answering the first question, and I mention it again because excitement is a good thing. Imagine the enjoyment of watching these kids having fun going to church and Sunday school. It surely beats what the world has to offer.

◆ God will bless your church for obeying the Great Commission. Your church will be doing more of what the church was commanded to do by our Lord.

◆ You will be helping the poor and the disadvantaged. We all love charitable work. The church is the greatest place there is for charitable work. We are meeting both the physical and spiritual needs of the bus riders.

◆ Families will be reached. One day you will see a family becoming active in the church, and you may wonder from where they came, only to discover that they were reached through the bus ministry.

◆ More people will have a place to serve the Lord. This can only help strengthen the church when more members are doing the work of the Lord.

What can I do? It is my experience that most Christians want to help and be a blessing. With that in mind, let me give you some things you can do to be a blessing to the bus ministry.

◆ Pray! Prayer will not only bring the blessings of God to the ministry, but it will also give you a more tender heart to the bus ministry.

◆ Have a good attitude. If someone starts to say something negative, deflect it with something positive. Never allow anyone to point out the problems without your pointing out the blessings. Be totally supportive.

◆ Be kind to these new attendees. Smile at them and make them feel welcome. Treat the dirtiest child as kindly as you would the most sophisticated adult.

◆ Give joyfully. When you tithe, a portion of that tithe will be used to pay the costs of operating buses. Designate weekly or monthly an extra amount to the bus ministry. Give in the special bus offerings.

◆ Encourage the bus workers. Let them know you appreciate their ministry and that you are praying for them.

◆ Overlook the inconveniences "as unto the Lord." Think of the inconveniences so many have made throughout history and are making even today to get out the Gospel to the world. Enjoy those inconveniences as a way you can do your part for the sake of souls.

◆ Volunteer to help occasionally. There will be big days when your church will need a few extra workers. Lend a hand. The blessings you will receive will be well worth the effort.

◆ Love these children. Look at them through eyes of compassion, understanding that for many of them your church will be the only hope they have. Some come from unloving and sin-infested home lives. Show them the love of Christ.

You may never drive or ride a church bus. You may never go out on bus visitation. You may not ever feel led to be involved in the bus ministry in any way. That does not mean that there will no rewards for you in Heaven. Only by the combined cooperation and efforts of the church family can a ministry such as this be totally effective and successful. You are an important part of this and every other ministry of your church. Remember this marvelous passage of Scripture as your church moves forward, and take it deeply to heart.

"For as the body is one, and hath many members, and all the members of that one body, being many, are one body: so also is Christ."—I Cor. 12:12.

"That there should be no schism in the body; but that the members should have the same care one for another."—I Cor. 12:25.

LEADING YOUR CHURCH TO SUPPORT THE BUS MINISTRY

YOU KNOW it is the right thing to do. God has spoken to your heart and given you the vision to start reaching out more in your area with the Gospel. You have thought about it, prayed about it, and even sought counsel about it; and now you are ready to start. How do you help your church members to catch the same vision you have for starting a bus ministry in your church?

Perhaps you have had a bus ministry for some time, but it has been stagnant for a long time with no real emphasis on it. The people never even think about it, but you have come to realize that it is time to take it to the next level. What can you do to revive the spirit for the bus ministry in your church?

Good men often approach me to ask questions such as these. They sincerely want to make the bus ministry a vibrant part of their churches, but they are not certain how to get the people involved and behind their decision. Let me share with you how to lead your church to the place where the bus ministry is one of the exciting ministries of your church and one that almost everyone will support.

1. Present the Need. What is the need? That is where it all begins. You must be sure you understand what the need is.

- ◆ The need is to reach the next generation with the Gospel.

+ The need is to reach and influence your area with God's Word.

+ The need is to win more souls to Christ.

+ The need is to obey Christ's commands to preach the Gospel to every creature.

+ The need is to go into the highways and hedges and bring them in.

A pastor must make certain that he knows the need and shares the need with his people. Preach the need. Bring the need before your people in your sermons. This will set the stage for announcing your decision. Don't just announce you are going to do it and expect them to do it because you happen to have a burden.

2. Present the Possibilities. The good that comes from the ministry far outweighs the challenges but sometimes is not as obvious. Let your people know of the blessings of having a bus ministry. Borrow stories from churches like ours who have been in the bus ministry and let your people know the great blessings in store by having a bus ministry.

3. Present the Potential. The potential is souls being saved. That is the bottom line of any ministry. Show your people the fact that more souls will be saved through the bus ministry than by any other means. Dollars invested in the bus ministry net greater spiritual returns than those invested almost any-where else. Get your people's mission-mindedness to extend to more than the foreign fields. Help them to realize that there are unharvested fields near your church. There are neighborhoods where no one is preaching the true Gospel. They may have the social gospel or the prosperity gospel, but many have no true soul-winning ministry anywhere near them. Your church can see many saved by going into those fields.

4. Present the Opportunity to Give. The Bible tells us that our hearts follow our treasures. Once the people have the burden, take special offerings for the new bus routes you are starting. Once people give to something, it becomes theirs. They take own-ership of it. Let them have the honor of giving, and they will be on board.

5. Present the Opportunity to Serve. Pastor, sometimes we make the mistake of thinking people want to come to church to observe and be ministered to. That could not be further from the truth. People want to serve. They want to be a part of the ministry of the church. Most churches have plenty of people involved in ushering or working in the nurseries. We have people who want to serve in a place where they can exercise their abilities for the Lord. That is what the bus ministry allows people to do. It is a place for people who really want to do a work for God. Take advantage of it by opening up this opportunity to people who need a place to serve the Lord.

6. Present the Results. From the beginning, share the blessings with the people. Has it ever dawned on us that if our people give, they probably would enjoy knowing about the eternal results that are taking place? We tell them when the mortgage is retired. We tell them when we make budget or don't. We tell them how much we raised for foreign missions or for a school campaign. Tell them the blessings of the bus ministry. Let them know of the blessings and share in the joy.

7. Present Examples. Conferences are a wonderful method to rekindle our spark or in some cases light a new fire. Take a few of your key folks, laymen as well as staff, to a bus conference and let them see the passion of those who are active in the ministry. When we as leaders attend, we come back with excitement and expanded vision and then expect our people to act upon that. Let them catch the vision by being a part of a good bus conference. It will electrify your church. On the Sunday night after the conference, let them share what God did for them. It is one thing when the pastor promotes the bus ministry. It is quite another when a layman does.

8. Present Patiently. No matter how good a job we do sharing all of the good there is in having a bus ministry, some will catch on slowly. Don't beat them up. Don't make them feel like second-class citizens. Give them time. They will catch on in time.

9. Present It Prayerfully. In everything we seek to do we must depend on the Lord to reach the hearts of the people. Bathe this new ministry in prayer. Pray! Nothing is more vital than that.

◆ Pray for it privately.

- ◆ Pray for it with your staff.
- ◆ Pray for it with your leadership.
- ◆ Pray for it publicly.

Pastor, you will love the blessings that will come to your church. Do what you must do to help your people get the heart for this great ministry. You will be glad you did, and in eternity you will know you did the right thing.

WHEN SHOULD YOU START A BUS MINISTRY?

THE BUS ministry is one of the greatest soul-winning tools available for reaching children and teenagers in your area. I love the bus ministry and have been a part of it for over thirty years. People often ask me when a church should start a bus ministry. I believe there are some basic principles to follow to help you know when and how to get a bus ministry started. There are three things to consider before starting a bus ministry. They are:

Finances (money)

Facilities (buildings or room)

Faculty (workers)

Some leaders teach that a church should have an attendance of at least a hundred or even a couple of hundred before starting a bus ministry. Some recommend that a church should maintain a ratio of seventy percent drive-in crowd and thirty percent bus crowd, or perhaps sixty/forty. Others recommend that it is best to wait two or three years after starting your church or becoming the pastor of a church to start running bus routes.

All of these may be good recommendations, but they still may fall short in fully guiding you as to the best time to begin. I believe there are some basic principles that can help you know when and how to get a bus ministry started in your church.

First, we know that the Great Commission is a threefold commandment. We are to

- ◆ win people to Christ;
- ◆ baptize our converts;
- ◆ teach them to observe or follow the instructions of the Bible.

These are all accomplished by personal soul winning, bringing our converts to church, and teaching them in Sunday school and church services.

Obeying the Great Commission is the main emphasis and the very purpose of our churches. The heartbeat of God is to reach the lost with the Gospel of the Lord Jesus Christ. **We are to reach everyone** we can with the message of salvation; and that includes children, teenagers and adults of all ages. Winning souls should be our passion, our burning desire, our heartbeat. People should be getting saved and baptized each week. The bus ministry is a great tool to accomplish that. It is the difference between fishing with one pole and casting a net over a multitude of fish.

I remember growing up in the mountains of southeastern Kentucky. I went down by the river and cut down cane for fishing poles. We laid those long poles on top of an outside building so that they could dry. Then I would wrap the fishing line around the end of one and tie on a hook and sinker. I would go searching for some big, fat, red worms to use for bait. Then I went fishing! I loved catching fish with those cane poles. In fact, I would bait up several of those poles and cast the line. Then I would stick the ends of the poles in the dirt on the riverbank so that I could have several lines and hooks in the water at the same time.

A few years later I bought a few rods and reels, and my fishing went to a whole new level. Eventually, I purchased a fishing boat so that my family and I could enjoy going further out where more fish (especially Crappie) were just waiting to be caught. We caught a lot of fish in that boat.

Now think of this. If all I had was a cane pole with which to fish, then that is what I used. I wanted to catch fish so I used what I had. When I could afford two poles, I used two poles. When I could afford a boat and a net, then I used them. If I could afford dynamite, then…(just kidding!). The point is, I used as much as I could to catch as many fish as I could.

When I became a pastor, at times I was the only one who went soul winning. As I won others to Christ, I was to take them soul winning with me and train them to win souls. Eventually we had enough people in church who were giving and winning souls that we were able to buy a bus to begin reaching children for Christ by "the bunches." As the church grew, even more and more people were giving and winning souls; we were able to buy more buses plus had more workers to work those buses.

Today we continue to grow and add bus routes. As of this writing we have twenty-four bus routes reaching and winning young people for Christ. Our primary purpose as a church is to win more people to Christ, see more of them baptized, and then to teach them the Word of God. Make no mistake about it: we did not start bus routes to build a church, but we built bus routes as the church grew.

If you follow this pattern, you will build a balanced church and be able to build more routes to reach more people. There are some important things to consider as you start a bus ministry: training workers, purchasing a bus, having the right kind of insurance, fuel for the buses, maintenance and other things. These and others will be covered throughout this book, but for now I want to encourage you to make it a goal to have a bus ministry—or to expand the one you have—so that you can reach more souls for Christ.

SHORT-TERM CHALLENGES VERSUS LONG-TERM RESULTS

A S BUS ministries begin to grow, so do the challenges that accompany them. Sadly, some men see the challenges; and rather than addressing them with solutions, they abandon the bus ministry entirely. In doing so they miss out on bountiful blessings they could enjoy. That is like a couple's giving up on having children merely because of the challenges that they bring. I would hate to have missed out on the great joys of having kids merely because they created challenges to my wife and me.

Likewise, I would hate to think of the blessings we would have missed as a church had we not had a bus ministry. These blessings include

- ◆ souls saved by the hundreds and thousands,
- ◆ lives changed,
- ◆ families reached and now driving to church together,
- ◆ bus workers who once were bus kids,
- ◆ workers in almost every ministry reached through our bus ministry,
- ◆ bus captains who once were bus riders now reaching children,
- ◆ preacher boys who were reached on the buses,
- ◆ soul winners who were reached through the bus ministry.
- ◆ people faithfully attending Sunday and Wednesday

nights who first came on buses.

That is merely a sampling of what we would have missed. By no means, however, should we ignore the challenges, nor do I plan to pretend they do not exist. As our bus ministry grew, three main problems accompanied that growth:

1. space issues

2. behavior problems

3. too many children to handle in a single service

Let me deal with these by telling you what we did at Clays Mill Road Baptist Church. These problems were dealt with in one basic method. We divided up our bus ministry first into two and later into three sections.

◆ We have several buses that bring children to our main drive-in Sunday school, and they attend the morning service once they are old enough to do so. Until that time they attend a children's church service.

◆ A second group of buses arrive fifteen minutes after our morning service has begun. They immediately attend Sunday school, and then they have their own church services.

◆ A third group of buses arrive in the afternoon; and using the same facilities, they have their Sunday school and church services.

By doing this we were able to accomplish several things.

1. Use our facilities more efficiently. Instead of using a Sunday school room once, we now use it three times. Instead of building more buildings, we use what we have in a better way.

2. Work with smaller groups of children at a given time. The bus ministry is a kids-intensive ministry. Having their services in sections allows us to have a balanced focus. Our first Sunday school and church service look pretty much like any other fundamental church services would look with a good mix of children, teenagers and adults. The next two are filled with far more children. We want to reach these kids, and dividing them into smaller groups makes it easier to do so.

3. Work with children with similar challenges. Some bus

routes are in areas where the discipline of the children is a greater problem. These children have had little to no training at home. They often come from broken homes or where the parents are alcoholics and/or drug users. This creates several issues.

- ◆ Some kids show no respect to any authority.
- ◆ Some have to be bribed to do anything at all.
- ◆ Some can even be destructive in their behavior.

Do we merely throw these kids away, or do we try to reach them? If the church gives up on them, what hope do they have? The world puts violence in front of them and mind-altering drugs inside them, and they are left with little hope of becoming productive adults. We must get the Spirit of God in them by introducing them to the Lord Jesus Christ. We must find a way to do this. We have seen what God can do with these children when the church refuses to give up on them. Good things begin to happen, and many graduate into the main church as they grow in the Lord.

Many years ago when Dr. Hyles first started the Chicago bus routes, his goal was to use these routes as a tool of service for the students of Hyles-Anderson College. The original plan for the "B" Sunday School was to have a graded Sunday school program going on during the main preaching service and then send these Chicago bus riders to the main auditorium for their own separate service, their second service.

The story goes that after only one week, Dr. Hyles realized this was not such a good idea. First, the workers were trying to get these first-time-church-attending kids into the auditorium while the main service was dismissing The bedlam that ensued was a logistical nightmare. Second, some of these kids were from gangs in the inner city. They did not mix well with the others. Then, too, when church began, it became apparent to Dr. Hyles that he was not going to have much success preaching to a couple thousand Chicago bus kids in that setting.

Within a week he had entirely reorganized the program into one that became a model of success. Rather than bringing the bus children in for one giant service, he had them go to many smaller church services near their Sunday school areas. What started out as a problem became a success story. Thousands of those bus kids became fine Christians and have circled the globe serving the Lord.

4. Expand our outreach and influence for Christ. There are so many places near most of our churches that need to be reached with the Gospel, but we limit ourselves because of lack of creative vision. D. L. Moody looked beyond the standard way things were done and as a result made a profound impact on a wicked city. Many others have done the same thing. The inner cities of this nation need what we teach and preach. Our country suffers because many inner-city people have no real gospel influence. Many churches could do something about such problems if they would follow these simple ideas.

"But what about workers?" I am often asked. "Who will work with these kids and give up their Sunday church time?"

I cover in more detail the subject of recruiting and enlisting workers in several later chapters in this book; however, there are a couple of facts I want to share here. The secret to an extended outreach is an extended vision. The pastor with a vision will find people with a vision. Do not furnish excuses for your people who could become your workers. Show me a pastor with a vision to reach out to more children, and I will show you a church where God brings adults with the passion to reach those kids. Do not think for your people. God raises up people to go to the hardships of third world countries to preach the Gospel. Why would He not raise up workers to reach the unreached in your area?

We make excuses far too often because we are scared. We see the challenges and think they are reasons not to do something. Be a man of God who sees the challenges and believes that God did not put you in your city to reach the fruit on the bottom limbs. He expects you to find a ladder tall enough to reach that which seems out of reach. The people will be there when your vision and commitment are sufficient to cause you to go to them.

Overcoming Hindrances
to Growth

IT IS EASY to become passive about things over which we feel we have no control. Churches that are not growing often became complacent out of frustration more than anything else. I truly believe that there are many pastors who would like their churches to grow but they just don't know what to do about some challenges they face. These good men come to me with their questions. They say things like:

- ◆ "We just do not have enough workers to reach everyone we could in the bus ministry."
- ◆ "We have run out of space for growth."
- ◆ "I just can't seem to get the people motivated."
- ◆ "The finances are not there to do all I would like to do."

These are what I call hindrances to growth. We all have them now or have had them at some time in the past. The struggling pastor often thinks he is a failure, or perhaps he has the wrong priorities and as a result gives up on growth. It is not that he is quitting; but if growth is impossible, then changing priorities is the alternative. Having been a pastor now for over twenty years and having counseled with many frustrated pastors, I feel there are a few things I have learned that may help you to overcome these hindrances.

First of all, please understand that hindrances are challenges that are often there to make us stronger. Bodybuilders will tell you that strength and muscle are developed by resistance. It is the resistance of the weight against the muscle that is actually increasing one's strength. The same is true with spiritual strength. There is, however, another strength often forgotten; and that is ministerial strength. The more resistance or hindrances I have endured, the more strength I have built up to overcome and resolve them. Do not resent these hindrances, for they will prepare you to overcome even more as your work grows bigger for the Lord.

The hindrance or challenge most often brought up by pastors is that of not having enough workers. You are going to find that I deal with this subject often because it is so prevalent. Space is another one that many pastors mention. Pastor, it may come as a surprise to you that Jesus was faced with the exact same challenges as we are.

"And Jesus went about all the cities and villages, teaching in their synagogues, and preaching the gospel of the kingdom, and healing every sickness and every disease among the people.

"But when he saw the multitudes, he was moved with compassion on them, because they fainted, and were scattered abroad, as sheep having no shepherd.

"Then saith he unto his disciples, The harvest truly is plenteous, but the labourers are few;

"Pray ye therefore the Lord of the harvest, that he will send forth labourers into his harvest."—Matt. 9:35–38.

It is quite obvious in this passage that Jesus did not have enough workers for the harvest. He was working hard. He was doing His best, yet here we see His "frustration" at the fact that there were not enough volunteers to do the work. Is that not a bit encouraging in and of itself? Jesus had our problem. That should not surprise us because, after all, He was tempted in every way we are. The difference was in His response to the problem.

We have the same problems today. We do not have as many workers as we need. Some of us do not have enough room or parking, and some do not have enough leaders. We have **most** of these problems much of the time at Clays Mill Road Baptist Church, but we see them as good problems. I would rather have the need than become stagnant. We have many workers, but we do not have anywhere near enough to reach our entire city and area for Christ. How do we deal with this? What are we going to do?

1. **If you do not have this problem, your vision is too small.** I have to begin here. I have never met a pastor who loved the lost and had a passion for his city who was not a bit frustrated. Hindrances are not hindrances to the one with a vision. They are challenges to find a way to do more. Not having enough space for the crowd surely beats not having enough crowd for the space.

2. **Be innovative.** Space is a problem for many growing churches. The temptation is to do away with smaller classrooms and have one giant assembly. While this may at times be the only solution, it is by no means the best one. Try to use some innovative ideas.

◆ Have table classes in a gymnasium or bigger assembly room. A restaurant has many tables where small groups are eating. There are many conversations taking place at the same time, yet it works because all in the same conversation are gathered around the same table. It works in Sunday school as well. We currently have twelve Sunday school classes that meet in our gymnasium.

◆ Buy or make folding partitions to divide up classes.

◆ Use buses for classrooms. While this may not be the best situation, it is better than not reaching children at all.

◆ Use offices for classrooms. High school classes meet more successfully in offices than do younger children's classes. If possible, it may be best if the teacher of the class is the person to whom the office belongs. It can be prepared and arranged according to his likes. This is better than allowing someone else to move or mess up things that do not belong to him.

◆ Have classes on stairways, in the baptism dressing areas, or anywhere you can find a space big enough to conduct a class of ten or so children. Make an adventure out of it. Kids will love it.

◆ Have a chair shortage? No problem. Use rugs and sit on

the floor. You can actually fit more kids into a smaller space that way.

3. Alternate the times your buses arrive for Sunday school and church. Currently we have groups arriving at five different times so that we can use the same classrooms multiple times in a day. Sunday morning we have the drive-in Sunday school at 10:00 and church at 11:00. When our church service begins, another set of buses arrive and use the same rooms that were used in the previous hour. The Spanish arrive at another scheduled time and once again use the same facilities. We have another set of bus routes that leave the church at 1:30 to pick up children. They use the buildings from 3:00 until 5:00 in the afternoon.

At present we have seating in our church auditorium for about 700. By using this rotating schedule, we are capable of reaching an attendance of up to 2,000. All of this takes work and planning, but we must be innovative and positive in our schedules and programs if we want to reach the harvest before us.

4. On a consistent basis, pray and preach for more workers. Notice what Jesus did. He not only prayed about it, but He made certain His disciples were aware of the need and admonished them to pray concerning it. Certainly we must be patient, using the workers God has given us at the time. This is what Jesus did. At the same time He told His disciples to pray for more laborers. We must do the same thing while still being thankful and excited about those who are already serving with us. We must stay positive and encouraging to the people who are already faithful in their places of service.

> **Note:** It is important to have the right workers in the right areas. I fear that we often use unqualified workers to start programs. They not only fail to accomplish the work but also create problems which altogether prevent bus routes, classes or a ministry from succeeding. It is imperative that we use qualified people and train those people on a regular basis for their part in the ministry.

More is said about this matter of recruiting and enlisting workers in several other chapters.

5. Have "brainstorming" meetings to discuss growing pains. Meet with your workers and seek their ideas on how to accommodate more people. You may be surprised at their ideas, but you will also make them more aware of the need to keep finding ways to grow and reach more people.

6. Stay positive and believe that you can grow. Do not make or accept excuses for not growing. You can grow! Being positive and excited is a decision you as a leader must make. Do not allow negative people to affect your thinking. A negative attitude makes it impossible to think of new ideas to solve challenges.

7. New converts are eager to be trained to serve. I love new Christians. Often they are the best source for new workers because they just want to do anything they can to serve the Lord. Have a special meeting and invite people to come who would like to get involved in a ministry of the church. Make certain new converts know they are especially welcome. Prepare a list of specific areas of need. Ask them to check the ones they feel may interest them. Contact them personally and begin the process of enlisting and equipping them.

8. Keep well organized that which you have. Frustration often leads to letting down the standard. Don't get stagnant, no matter how difficult your situation may seem. Stay on top of things now as you prepare for future growth.

I have dealt primarily with space challenges. Throughout this book I will address other hindrances and challenges in more detail. Make a decision that you will be a ministry overcomer and not a victim of your circumstances.

II

THE
PEOPLE OF THE
BUS MINISTRY

THE WORKERS ON
A BUS ROUTE

HAVING THE right workers on a bus route is such an important aspect of having a good bus ministry. In the years working on and with bus routes, I have come to appreciate the role of every worker. A bus route cannot function without these volunteers who give of themselves to help reach children and their families for Christ. Here are a few thoughts about these workers.

- ◆ They should be qualified for their jobs.
- ◆ They should have defined duties.
- ◆ They should be properly trained to fulfill those duties.
- ◆ They should be allowed to do their jobs.
- ◆ They should be good team players.
- ◆ They should know their importance and your appreciation for them.

A good bus route is a well-oiled machine where everyone and everything work smoothly and in harmony. It is a team where everyone knows what he is supposed to be doing and what the other workers are doing. They pull together and make each Sunday a success in every way. Allow me briefly to describe the different jobs on a bus route.

1. The captain. Everything rises and falls on leadership in any organization, and it is true with a bus route. The bus captain is the general, the pastor, the leader, and the one responsible for making certain the bus route is run properly. He must know everything that is going on and make certain that everything is running smoothly. A good captain is good at many things including delegating responsibility to other workers. If the captain does this, he will be free to do whatever else needs to be done.

2. The driver. That is what he does: he drives the bus. He also is in charge of making certain all laws are obeyed and that every safety precaution is taken. He is the captain of the ship and stays with the bus at all times. More is covered in detail on this vital position in another chapter.

3. The secretary. This person should keep all the records, including registration forms with accurate information about each child, along with signatures from his parent(s). Keeping an attendance log is also an important duty of the bus secretary.

4. The runner. This person runs to the door to let them know the bus is there and accompanies the riders to the bus. Once on the bus the runner can also be in charge of making certain their hands are stamped. Then on the bus ride home, the runner escorts the riders to their front doors, making certain they are properly inside with their parents.

5. The program/song leader. This could be more than one person because you may assign different parts of the program to different workers. It is a good idea to have one person who is in charge of the bus program to make certain it keeps flowing along with no gaps. Nothing will hurt more than a busload of kids not having fun. The program leaders keep things moving on the bus.

6. The helpers. These unsung heroes are vitally important on the bus route. They do a little bit of everything.

- Befriend riders
- Participate enthusiastically in the program
- Encourage riders
- Keep riders under control
- Help with discipline
- Break up spats among riders (that sometimes happen)

- Keep the bus clean
- Keep windows up
- Help keep everyone safe
- Give out prizes and promotional treats
- Clean up messes
- Escort kids to Sunday school classes
- Pick up younger kids at Junior church
- Anything else the bus captain needs done

Do not assume anything or take anything for granted. It is in the tiniest details that victories are won or, sadly, where we lose or have tragedy. Each worker has a job to do; and if everyone does his job with the right attitude and with the Spirit of God in his life, the blessings of God will flow.

THE RIGHT TIMING IN GETTING
A BUS DIRECTOR

PASTORS OFTEN ask me how to pick a good bus director and when they should consider doing so. I believe this is important because if you pick the wrong man or pick the right man too soon, you may end up hurting the ministry or even the man himself. Timing is important because as the bus ministry grows, so too do the responsibilities of leading it.

The pastor often has his hands full with all the duties of the church, and the bus ministry can be a time-intensive ministry. That said, don't give it away just because you are tired of doing it yourself. For awhile before getting a bus director, you may want to assign to others some of the duties pertaining to details, while at the same time maintaining the leadership of the ministry yourself; but there will come a time when you must get a bus director. Pastors often ask these three questions:

1. **Now or later?** "When is the right time to hire a bus director?" I will give you a very simple answer, but first let me state that your being tired of handling it is not a good reason to give it to someone else. Here is a simple rule of thumb: when the needs of your people are not being met because of the magnitude of time and attention being demanded by the bus ministry, you should begin considering finding a man to help you.

You are called to be the pastor of the church, and that entails many things. When your church is small, you'd better be a hard worker, or God will never use you to build a great work. Leading the bus ministry for a time will help you better to understand it in the future. It may not be a permanent task, but do not feel sorry for yourself if you must lead it for a time. Enjoy it and develop a passion for it.

Do not make it an excuse for not growing. I believe that a pastor can be the bus director in a growing church. I have done it. Often we get lazy and want to find someone else to do what we do not want to do because of the size of the commitment involved. That is a huge mistake. Wait until the time is right and you have found the right man to take your place. Until then, do it yourself.

2. Staff or layman? This can be a difficult question to answer because every situation is different. Let me ask you a question: If you paid someone to lead every ministry of your church, how would that affect your budget? Often we take the easy way of hiring someone when perhaps financially we are not ready.

Dr. Hyles was a master of having laymen lead ministries. His choir director for years was a layman and was paid a small salary for his work with the choir.

I have been very fortunate to have a man who was capable of leading our growing bus ministry as a layman while maintaining his full-time job. That has been a perfect situation for us. He attends staff meetings. He treats it like a full-time job, but it is not. Be careful. Not every layman is capable of doing this. However, perhaps there is a layman who could begin part-time and eventually be full-time as your bus director. Be careful about giving and taking away titles. If you feel this is temporary, make certain he understands and agrees with you. Later you may hurt him if you replace him with someone else. One good way to find out if a man has the qualities needed to be a bus director is to make him your assistant bus director at first.

Another danger is hiring a man based upon your hopes rather than your needs. Some men take a church with a vision of growth. Then they hire a staff of men to produce that growth. Beware, Pastor. That is usually a recipe for disaster. I hire to assist with the growth we are having rather than to stimulate the growth we are not having. There is a difference between a need and a wish. Hire for needs, not wishes.

3. Full-time or part-time? There are times when a bus ministry is growing but is not in need of a full-time man to lead it. Perhaps you could assign the duty to another staff man who has time to take on a bit more responsibility, as long as his existing duties do not conflict. In a growing young church, it is sometimes a good idea to let a man grow with and into the position. Few things are worse than hiring a man into full-time position in a ministry that does not need him full time. Then you spend your time trying to find other things for him to do. In many churches the bus man is also the visitation director or youth director or even a Christian school teacher or administrator. If you as pastor are leading it with all of your other various duties, then it may be a good idea to start a man off part time.

The next two chapters are going to deal further with the qualities and responsibilities of a bus director. Before moving on to these, let me conclude this chapter by suggesting that you not wait until you need him to find the right man. Your search should begin now because you want to be in a search mode all the time. There may be a man in your ministry now who is already loyal to you and the work of the church and who could someday be very capable of leading your bus ministry. So, he did not go to Bible college. He is in the best place for training he could be as he works with you in the ministry of the local church. Some of the greatest leaders in churches have been men who never went off to college.

Pick your leaders well, Pastor. Precious souls are at stake.

RESPONSIBILITIES OF A BUS DIRECTOR

IN MANY churches the leadership of the bus ministry rests upon the shoulders of the pastor. For many years I was privileged to be the pastor of the church as well as to direct the work of the bus ministry. As the church grows and the demands increase, there will come a time when the pastor will need to relinquish some of his duties. One area which he may want to assign to another is directing the work of the bus ministry. Whether it is the pastor or another who leads, there must be some guidelines that help the leader to know what this entails.

1. **Lead in carrying out the Great Commission.** A bus director's main purpose is to get people saved, baptized and in church so that they can grow in the Lord. The purpose is not to have a bigger attendance, although that certainly will be a by-product. His main purpose is not to please the pastor, although pleasing the pastor is not a bad thing. The mind-set must always be on carrying out the Great Commission. That is his job first and foremost.

2. **Understand the overall picture of the church and its ministries.** Many churches are hurt when a leader of a ministry places his personal best interest above the overall welfare of the church. The bus ministry is a part of the overall ministry and must operate as part of the team. He must see himself as a fellow laborer with those in other ministries, like soul-winning groups, Sunday school, nursing home ministry, children's groups, etc. No ministry stands alone or is exclusive of the others in the work

of the team. On a football team a quarterback without a receiver and linemen is not going to succeed. Every ministry and every ministry worker is vital to the success of all others. There are few ministries which overlap more with other ministries than does the bus ministry.

3. Know and subsequently convey the heart of the pastor to the people. It may seem strange that I would include this in the list of duties, but I believe it is very appropriate to do so. A leader of a church ministry such as the bus ministry must study the pastor and know what his vision is for the church. The bus director should

 ◆ ask the pastor many questions when he meets with him;

 ◆ listen carefully to his sermons;

 ◆ attend as many meetings as he can to learn what the pastor is doing;

 ◆ attend Sunday school teachers' meeting to know the pastor's heart regarding the Sunday school;

 ◆ let the pastor know that he wants to be in tune with his heart; ask the pastor please to let him know if he sees an area where he is not in tune with him; tell him if such an area is found, he wants to make adjustments;

 ◆ take all suggestions and criticisms with a positive and grateful attitude; not get defensive.

4. Plan and organize promotions. More will be said in other chapters regarding promotions, but suffice it here to say that the bus director must be good at carrying out promotions and big days.

5. Recruit and enlist workers. Again, this is something that will be taught in more detail, but the bus director must be proactive in this area. He should not wait until he needs workers to recruit them. This is a 365-day-a-year responsibility.

6. Organize and carry out the day-to-day work of the bus ministry. There are many details involved with operating a bus ministry. Those details should fall on the shoulders of the bus director and not be left for the pastor to handle.

 ◆ Forms and flier preparation

- Ordering promotional items
- Bus repairs
- Insurance matters
- Reading and responding to bus reports

7. **Solve problems as they arise.** Problems will arise on a weekly basis in any ministry but especially the bus ministry. If the bus director procrastinates in dealing with them, they will only grow and may even create more problems. The bus director should not hide problems from the pastor, but he should not allow them to grow until the pastor must handle them.

8. **Oversee the safety and mechanical concerns of the buses.** Again, being proactive is of the utmost importance. Bus workers get very discouraged if week after week the bus is not ready and in good working order. Breakdowns will occur, but the bus director must do everything he can to minimize these problems.

9. **Conduct the bus meeting each Saturday.** This is a very important duty for the bus director because that meeting will set the tone for the entire work of the bus ministry. More will be said in another chapter about conducting a bus workers' meeting, but the director must make it his responsibility to see to it that every week the meeting is done properly.

10. **Be sure bus workers have all the items they need to run their routes.** Nothing will destroy a bus route and ministry faster than not having the things you promised for promotions or not having enough fliers and forms. The bus director must be prepared.

11. **Communicate with the workers throughout the week.** Accessibility is vital. If the workers struggle reaching the bus director, they will become disheartened and may lose trust in him. If they cannot get through to him, they will begin to bypass him and go to the pastor instead. That should not happen. With all the digital communication available to us today, there should never be difficulty getting in touch with the bus director.

12. **Keep the pastor informed of what is going on within the bus ministry, both the good and the bad.** He should take problems to the pastor not to be solved but with a solution

already in hand. The pastor should never be blindsided by an issue because of the carelessness of the bus pastor to inform him. Communicate with memos, emails, text messages; but let him know what is happening.

13. Look for new areas for potential routes. Growth is essential because there are many who need the Gospel. The bus director must keep his eyes open for areas where a bus route could be effectively started. In other words, he should have a vision.

14. Train the workers. Training is a big key to success. The bus director must have a good program of training in place. Do not allow training to be done carelessly. Training should be detailed, intense, ongoing, and repetitive. Each worker—captain, driver, helper—must be trained.

Many of these areas of responsibility need more elaboration and will be covered in greater detail in this book. This is, however, a snapshot view of what a bus director's duties should entail. The job is not an easy one, but it is doable with the Lord's enablement. The bus director must be strongly committed to being successful in reaching lives for Christ.

IMPORTANT QUALITIES OF A BUS DIRECTOR

SHOW ME A man of Christian character, and I will show you a man who can be trained to do the work God wants him to do. Often pastors make the mistake of seeking talent and ability and end up getting a person who is lacking in the qualities needed to be used of God. I am big on choosing leaders who possess the right qualities over men who have charming personalities or who are greatly talented. Here are the qualities for which I look in a bus director.

1. He must be a Spirit-filled Christian. This may seem like it should go without saying, but I cannot go without saying it because it is so important. In this position, a man without the guidance of the Holy Spirit is a sitting duck for attacks by Satan. Look at his life. Look at his family. Look at his soul-winning zeal. Watch his spirit. Go bus calling and soul winning with him and see if there is evidence that he is a man who walks in the Spirit. He may have the personality for which you are looking, but without the Spirit of Christ he will eventually fail.

2. He must possess a passion for souls. Reaching souls for Christ is the reason for the bus ministry. It is not merely for increasing your attendance for the sake of a bigger number. You may have someone who could get more people; but if he does not labor out of a heart that cares for the souls of boys and girls, his work will be for naught.

**3. He should love and fully grasp the potential of the bus ministry. We have all heard the saying, "You can't fit a square peg in a round hole." That is true with the bus ministry. If a man does not have the heart for it, he will be like a fish out of water. There has to be a passion within him for the ministry itself. He must believe that it is potentially the greatest soul-winning tool in the world.

4. He should be patient and flexible. A stubborn and quick-tempered man will be a disaster working as bus director. Issues will test him every week. Sundays can be trying with children creating problems and buses breaking down, all while he's trying to follow a multifaceted schedule. The man must be able to adjust and respond properly to any given situation.

5. He should have a burning desire to build an effective and successful bus ministry. It must become the passion, vision and heart of the bus director as well as of the pastor. If the bus director is not always showing the desire to do more, he will do less. Sometimes I have to hold a man back a bit, but that is far better than having to shove him forward.

6. He should be a good judge of the abilities and potential of people. Every ministry is concerning people. In ministering to the bus kids, the bus director must not forget that he is ministering to the workers as well. He cannot treat them like hired hands, because they are volunteers. Therefore, he must be able to discern what best fits them. In his haste to get workers, he must be willing to give away a worker to another ministry if he is better suited to it.

7. He should be a good motivator of people. A motivator is someone who knows how to put more fuel on the motive. We think motivating is manifested by giving a good pep talk or a prize. Those are important, but the most important thing is the motive. We stir hearts to visit more, stay faithful, love the kids, and do the work by pouring fuel on the fire of what caused the workers to get involved in the first place. Sometimes we lose sight of the main thing because we attempt to motivate people outside of the real motive. I contend that people join the bus ministry to please God and reach lives. Keep the motive hot and alive.

8. He should have the ability to get along with different kinds of people. We call this being a "people person," but really it is a matter of having wisdom more than it is anything else. A man with wisdom will be able to get along with and work with almost any type of person. That is vital in any growing and thriving ministry.

9. He should be able to work under pressure. This was mentioned in point number 4. Never forget that the pressure of a Sunday can be immense and intense. Some men thrive under pressure, and some do not. Choose a man who has calmness and the strength to be able to stand in pressured situations. You do not want a man who makes problems worse by the way he reacts.

10. He should be able to maintain a good spirit. As you read my writings on the work of the ministry or hear me preach, you will notice a distinct emphasis on spirit. That is because I have seen many ministries hurt by a bad spirit in a leader or worker. You cannot tell much about a man's spirit when everything is going his way. It is when he is tested or when he must deal with matters in a way that he may not prefer that you will really see what kind of a spirit he has.

I have known men who, the minute they were corrected, did a complete about-face in their attitude. Confrontation reveals the true spirit of a man. Be very certain that the man you place over this important ministry is a man whose spirit is good at all times. If he has never dealt with adversity, you cannot know how he will face it when it comes; but it will come.

11. He must be humble. Nothing is worse than an arrogant leader or a leader who feels that some task is beneath him. When I look for a leader, I watch how he handles the menial tasks. I want to know if he is willing to get his hands dirty in the trenches or if he merely puts it off on another. A bus director must be a strong man with a controlled ego.

12. He must be a problem solver. As I have said before, there will be problems. The bus director must be the kind of man who knows how to deal with problems in an effective and principled manner.

13. He must be loyal. This quality is not the last because it is of the least importance. That is by no means true. Loyalty should go without saying, but it is too important not to say it. The bus director has influence on a fairly large segment of the church. If you have a man who has his own agenda, he will cause you heartbreak like you have never known. If he puts the bus ministry above the church or any other ministry in the church, you will have problems. He must be loyal to the pastor, to the church and all its ministries, to his workers, and to the cause of Christ.

Once you have found a man with the right qualities, you have taken a very important step towards filling the need. However, take your time. Study the man carefully. Know the answers to any questions you may have about him before you give him the title and position. This is better than being surprised later.

THE BUS DIRECTOR, MOTIVATOR

MOTIVATION is a very important part of leadership. The root word of *motivation* is *motive*. What exactly is a motive? According to the dictionary, there are three different ways to define *motive*. Each of these is an important element of working with people.

1. Causing or able to cause motion. In short, this is the ability to get people to do something. Some can lead people to *thought,* but that is not leadership. Leaders know how to lead people to *action.*

2. Impelling to action. This is a very interesting definition because it means to drive people forward to do something for the sake of a cause. What is our cause? Souls are our cause, as well as changed lives.

3. Of or constituting an incitement to action. This is the ability to get people to thrust themselves behind a task. This is the type of motivation that causes a bus ministry to have a big day. People are stirred to do something extraordinary. A good leader can motivate people to reach goals they never thought they could reach.

A good bus director becomes good at motivating people to do what they are supposed to do, do what they ought to do, and do more than they thought they could do. The difference between motivation and manipulation is that motivators stir the emotions to *want to* do more; manipulators stir the emotions to feel they *have to* do more. Leaders must learn not to *shame* people to action but to *stir* them to action. While it may seem to be emotional stimulation, it comes from a real and principled burden for the lost.

1. We motivate with experience. The great motivators learn how to motivate with a hands-on style of leadership. Would you like to know how to motivate someone to win souls? Take him soul winning with you. Would you like to know how to motivate someone to visit? Take him visiting with you. Seeing is more than merely believing. Seeing is experiencing. Show people how to do things, and you will discover that they will be motivated by seeing your actions.

2. We motivate with excitement. I don't know about you, but I enjoy excitement. If I go to a ball game, I get caught up in the excitement and energy of the crowd. Have you ever wondered why there is such a thing as home field advantage? It is because the players are driven to do more when the crowd is cheering them on. We can get hyper-spiritual and say that people ought to do more merely because it is the right thing to do. That may be true, but being excited is also the right thing to do, and leaders need to learn this fact. Keep things exciting, and people will be motivated.

3. We motivate with leadership. A leader is one who knows how to treat people well and to show concern for their needs. Nothing de-motivates someone like a lack of organization or planning. The workers show up, and the buses are not ready. That de-motivates. The bus fliers are not done well, or there are not enough printed. That de-motivates. A motivator is not one who merely adds motivators. He is also one who removes de-motivators. A mom does her best to make the veggies tasty and appealing to motivate her children to eat them. Preparation is a wonderful motivator.

4. We motivate with spiritual principles. Never expect people always to be on top of their game. Get their hearts ready by reminding them of what is at stake and why you do what you do. We do what we do for many reasons, and we must remind our workers of these often.

 ◆ to obey the Lord by winning the lost

- to keep people out of Hell
- to reach boys and girls for Christ
- to lift the fallen
- to love the unloved
- to please the Lord

5. **We motivate with example**. This is by no means least important. Setting an example is the greatest motivator of all. Christ came not to dictate the law or abolish the law, but to fulfill the law. He is our example. We do what we do because of what He did. People will do more if we do more. They will sacrifice more if we sacrifice more. A leader fails when he arrives at a point where he feels he has earned the right to do less. Great leaders seek to do more, not less; and that is what motivates people to do more. They also motivate by being the embodiment of what they want their people to be:

- Spirit-filled;
- walking with God;
- having compassion for souls;
- living holy, separated lives.

6. **We motivate with making decisions**. People need a leader who "calls the play." Coaches call a timeout to motivate their team, but look on the sidelines during the timeout, and you will see a marker board in their hand. They are drawing out a play for the team to run. That is what leaders do. If we merely try to get people excited but they have no idea what to do, they will fail. Eventually our words of excitement will fall on deaf ears because they see no direction. Be a decision-maker, and people will be motivated to do more.

7. **We motivate with goals**. People love to reach the goals someone else sets for them, yet they themselves fear setting the goals. Your children will not set goals for themselves; but when you set them for them with positive possibilities, they will respond. People need to be winning. We were made to want to achieve, and there is nothing wrong with that. A good leader knows how to get people working harder because they are seeking to achieve something greater.

8. We motivate with rewards. Jesus was the greatest motivator of all. He also spoke often of the reward that would come for doing certain things. The Bible is a book filled with rewards. It speaks of rewards over a hundred times, yet some people criticize doing something for a reward. Why do you think God offers so many rewards? Because He wants to give to His people for two reasons: first, because He is good and He loves us. However, He also wants us to choose to do good so that He can reward us. You do the same thing in your home. Food is not a reward for doing good, but a piece of candy might be. You feed your kids because you love them. You reward them with candy because they obey or achieve a goal. Reward your workers and you will motivate them.

9. We motivate with love. Dr. Hyles said, "I want people to love me. I seek to make them love me but not because I need their love. If they love me, they will allow me to help them." Have you ever seen a losing team become a winning team for the sake of a new coach for whom they wanted to win? When people love and admire a leader, they want to do more for him. Leadership understands that from the time we are children, we seek to please those we love. Add this to that equation: we seek to be loved so that we can please. Also, people want someone they can love so that they will want to please him. We were made to please God and others.

10. We motivate with success. Failure leads to discouragement. Success leads to wanting more success. I know that there are dry times in our lives; but when victory comes, it makes us want to do more. One important duty of a leader is to set reasonable expectations of his people. I love setting goals, but I never want to set a goal that I think is unreasonable. If we work hard to hit a goal and miss it yet still have a great day, it is bittersweet. Success is measurable whether we believe it or not. Goals are not unspiritual. They are ways to help us see definitive accomplishment that excites us to do even more. When I work hard for God and see success, I want to work even harder.

Bus leader, be a motivator, and you will build a great ministry with people who are excited to serve with you. Master these areas of motivation, and you will see the fruits of your labor and enjoy leading your workers to greater success and blessings.

Suggestions for a New Bus Director

O FTEN a young pastor or a new bus director will ask me for advice regarding leading a bus ministry. Perhaps he is stepping into the church as pastor, and with this responsibility he is to lead the bus ministry; or perhaps he has recently been asked to assume the position of bus director for the church. I have been in his position; therefore, I can certainly understand the issues he is facing. Here are the things I believe a new bus director should do if he wants better to establish himself in his work.

1. **Get to know the ministry.** When you become the director of an established ministry, you want to be careful that you build on what is there rather than rebuilding or starting over. Even if the ministry is small, it is always good to have something upon which you can build.

   ◆ **Get to know the leaders.** Learn who your leaders or influencers are. Stay close to the people who lead others. Do not let personality be the basis of your relationships; rather, form relationships on the bases of character and desire to serve the Lord. Let them know you want them to connect you to their vision, desire, personality, love, and heart for serving the Lord.

   ◆ **Get to know the workers.** Here is where the rubber meets the road. These are the people that make it happen on a week-to-week basis. Take the time and have the interest to find out more about the people with whom you are serving. Be sure to establish an "open door" policy with your leaders and workers. They must know they have access to the pastor and the bus director. Get to know

- their testimony of salvation and start in the ministry;
- the years of service they have been involved;
- the areas of the ministry in which they are involved;
- their talents and abilities;
- their personalities and interests within the bus ministry (they are better suited with some personalities over others);
- their needs and burdens (wayward children, handicaps, personal illness);
- their ideas and suggestions.

♦ **Get to know the riders.** Visit in the homes of as many faithful bus kids and families as you can. Just stop by and spend a few minutes getting to know them. This will also help you to get a heart for the people. We have heard the statement, "People do not care how much you know until they know how much you care." You may learn of the strengths and weaknesses of the bus routes by listening to the riders and parents.

♦ **Get to know the area**. Let me recommend that you do this in three different ways.

- ♦ Drive the routes with your captains.
- ♦ Drive the area with the pastor or someone who knows the area well.
- ♦ Scope out potential future bus route areas.

2. **Do not focus on inherited problems.** Focus on your direction. Problems need to be addressed, but that cannot be our focus. Do not be critical of the condition of the bus ministry. You do not know the challenges yet, so be careful not to cast a negative light on the way things used to be done. Our focus must be on the future direction. Get excited and stay excited about building a work for God!!!

3. **Ask lots of questions without giving too many opinions.** The best way to learn all about the ministry you are taking is to ask people questions. Do not be a know-it-all. Come in humbly

and show a sincere interest in the ideas and concerns of others—the pastor, the captains, the workers, the riders, and the parents.

4. Copy successful bus directors and bus ministries. In every ministry I have ever led, I started out learning everything I could from those who were successfully doing what I was about to start. Again, do not be a know-it-all. There are great books, audios, videos, and publications that can give you help in your new position. Get to know other bus directors and build a relationship that would enable you to call them with questions. Go to bus conferences wherever you can. Be a student, and your workers will copy your example.

5. Laugh at your mistakes. Let your bus workers know that you do not take yourself too seriously and that you can laugh at yourself when you mess up—because you will mess up. Do not be so self-absorbed that you cannot admit mistakes. Others will admit their mistakes if they see you doing so first.

6. Get on a schedule. The people should know you are a hard worker, not merely a director. Get your time scheduled quickly and put it on paper. Let your schedule be your boss. Plan time off but not time that your people see. They need to know you are available when needed.

7. Make it apparent that you are there to serve. People will follow you if you are a servant/leader. Great leaders consider themselves as servants first. Let all know you are there for them, not them for you. From the very first day, get into the mode of being a servant—

- serve the Lord,
- serve the pastor,
- serve the church,
- serve the bus workers, and
- serve the bus riders and their families.

8. Be readily available. Accessibility is vital for any leader but especially for one whose ministry is in the formative stages. People cannot get to know you, nor you, them, if you are not available to and for them. Make it easy for them to contact you and to ask you questions. Do not isolate yourself or make people feel they can't reach you when they need something. In this day and age there are so many ways a leader can remain accessible—at the church, on the phone, by text or email.

9. Be optimistic and enthusiastic. Start positive and stay that way. People will want to be around you if you keep the right spirit and attitude.

- Never complain.

- Never have "the-cup-is-half-empty" attitude. Let your viewpoint be "the cup is half full."

- Never tell your problems or the problems of the ministry to your bus workers.

- Never criticize.

10. Be loyal from Day One and forevermore. Your ministry depends on your ability to be loyal and to inspire loyalty in others. True loyalty comes from the example of a leader, not his expectations. Never give cause for anyone to doubt your loyalty to the pastor or the other programs and leaders within the church. Let your people know that they can trust you to be loyal to them. If they hear you criticize another leader, they will know that you would criticize them as well.

New opportunities are exciting, and our doing the right things can lead to great blessings and success. It all depends on us and on how we handle the opportunity that God has allowed us to have.

THE MINISTRY OF THE BUS CAPTAIN

THE PASTOR or bus director has come to you with something that God has already been speaking to you about doing, but you really were not sure if it was the right thing or the right time. In your heart you know it is the right thing to do, but you want to make certain you are prepared for that which you are going to begin. You are about to become a bus captain.

There are no little jobs in the work of God, but there are some that require a tremendous amount of commitment and which carry with them a great deal of responsibility. Being a bus captain is one of those. You want to do a good job, so you want to make sure you know exactly what the responsibilities are for being a captain.

1. The captain is the shepherd of the bus route. This is a spiritual aspect of his job. Just as a pastor shepherds the flock, a bus captain is to be the same to his bus route. It is amazing how much the children on a bus route will look to their bus captain as a leader. A captain must be careful that he recognize the influence he has on these children's lives and be faithful to lead them. To some extent, he has the watch care of their eternal souls, their walk with God, their spiritual growth, and their safety from Satan's attacks.

2. The captain is the overseer of the route. This is the practical portion of his responsibility. The overseer is the guardian of the sheep. He oversees all aspects of their well-being. The bus captain does this on the bus route. He makes certain that everything is the way it should be on the route.

As pastor of the church, I oversee all things that happen within the church, not to be a dictator but to make certain all is done decently and in order. That is true of the bus captain in areas of his route, including things such as:

◆ the equipment—that is, the bus;

◆ the program;

◆ safety;

◆ the workers;

◆ the welfare of the riders; and

◆ the promotions.

3. The captain is the steward of the workers' time and talents. Those who volunteer their time to the bus ministry are in that ministry under the care and leadership of the bus captain. They need to be led and spiritually cared for. Captains who use their workers wrongly do not build effective routes and end up having a high turnover rate of workers. Workers want to be used of God, but they do not want to feel we are using them for our acclaim. Treat them as fellow laborers, not hired hands. We will face God for the way we treat those who serve with us in our ministries.

◆ Put them in the right place to fit their talents and gifts.

◆ Protect their time by not wasting it.

◆ Say "please" and "thank you."

◆ Show gratitude often and in abundance.

◆ Word commands to sound like requests.

◆ Pray for them.

◆ Care about their needs and burdens.

◆ Show Christlike love for them.

4. The captain is an extension of the pastor and bus director. The pastor and bus director lend strength to what you do if you learn to be their extension and not a renegade. Some people feel it is weak to obey and follow instruction. They could not be more wrong. The authority of others over you strengthens your credibility and authority.

◆ Point your workers and riders to the pastor and bus director.

◆ Learn to speak of them when you teach or instruct with words such as "The pastor always says...," or "The bus director told me the other day that we need to...."

◆ Never usurp their authority.

◆ Never make up your own policies or rules without permission.

◆ Never contradict their policies or principles.

◆ Never second-guess them.

◆ Never cast aspersion on them.

5. **The captain is the ambassador for Christ and the church to his community**. A church bus is a very visible thing. You can't hide it. People are watching you and wondering about you. After all, most churches don't send buses out to pick up people for church. You can have a testimony in your community that, over time, you will bring many to Christ. Always be aware of that fact.

◆ Be considerate of other drivers.

◆ Be considerate of the neighbors of your bus riders.

◆ When you are out on visitation, always greet people with a warm smile.

◆ Be compliant with the police officers or city officials you meet.

◆ If you are ever pulled over, do not be defensive. Thank them for the job they are doing and apologize if you made a mistake or even if they just think you did.

6. **The captain is an example and a leader**. These are joined together because you really cannot be one without being the other. A good example makes a good leader. Lead by example. "Show and tell" is something we all learned in school. Don't reverse the two by using "tell and show." Do what you want your workers and riders to do. Establish the pattern of good works;

and then when you teach them, they will be reminded that they have seen this in you. Teach by example these things:

- ◆ dress and grooming
- ◆ attitude of positivity
- ◆ excitement and enthusiasm
- ◆ calmness and patience in adversity
- ◆ faithfulness to the task and to your other Christian duties
- ◆ love for souls and lives of people
- ◆ humility and a servant's heart

You may be thinking, *That is a pretty overwhelming list for me to fulfill. Can I do this?* That leads to the final and most important ingredient you need.

7. The captain must depend upon the Lord. In all we do, we are often too quick to think that the task is all there is to it. That is not true in our work for God. We must recognize that what we do is spiritual, not carnal, so we really cannot do it without relying on Him. If you think you are not capable but you are willing to rely on the Lord to help you, well, maybe you really are ready to be a captain. Believe me, you won't regret it!

Pastor's Role in Getting
More People Involved

IT TAKES many people to operate any ministry in the church successfully, but in many churches the bus ministry involves more people than perhaps any other ministry. Bus routes require a good number of committed people to make certain they run safely and effectively. On the other hand, the bus ministry can be one of the least attractive ministries for many people. It requires a great deal of time and effort; therefore, many people will shy away from it and find other avenues where they can serve. They also may feel they could not be effective as a bus worker, so they opt for something they feel is less daunting.

Pastors and bus workers often ask me how to get more of their people involved in the bus ministry. In fact, often the main reason they are not expanding is that they lack workers. Recruiting and enlisting workers is something to which both the pastor and the bus workers must commit themselves all the time. The mistake many make is that they wait until there is a desperate need to get really serious about finding workers. They then end up either begging or browbeating people, and neither of those is an effective method.

A business executive once said, "I am always looking for more people even when I don't need more people because I want always to be prepared when the need arises."

The best situation for a pastor and bus captain is to have more workers than they need. My belief is that getting people involved in the bus ministry is not that difficult as long as you consistently follow a few principles and practices. In this chapter I am going to deal with things the pastor can do to enlist workers.

1. Promote it from the pulpit. What you emphasize to your people will be what they feel is important. Some pastors hide the bus ministry from their people almost like it is a covert operation that they don't really want to discuss. In the minds of the people in your church, the bus ministry is only as important as you make it. Do not cram it down their throats but make it visible. Speak of it. From time to time in your sermons use illustrations from the bus ministry. The pulpit is the place where the heart of the church is often determined.

2. Promote it in the church bulletin regularly. The bus ministry, including the opportunity and need for workers, should be mentioned in the church bulletin regularly. Let me point out that the word *need* is the word we often think will trigger someone to volunteer. However, there are people who would be more likely to do so when they recognize an opportunity to serve. Many are looking for a way to serve. For example, you may be looking for drivers. Instead of printing "Drivers needed," perhaps you could word it something like this: "Do you have a CDL license? We have an opportunity for those with CDL licenses to serve the Lord in the bus ministry." Give them a way to contact someone, and you may be surprised that people may step up to the plate. Wording in the bulletin should appeal both to need and opportunity.

3. Have a bus update in the Sunday evening service. This is something that can have a huge impact on your people. Allow a bus teenager to give a testimony of what God has done in his life because of the bus ministry. You may want to bring a bus captain up to the platform and have him tell of a great victory on his route. You may even ask an exceptional worker to give a word as to the blessing of the bus ministry in his life. It may be wise to interview the person rather than just giving him the microphone and freedom to say whatever comes to his mind. Having testimonies allows everyone to experience the good that is taking place as a result of the bus ministry.

4. Use public praise and recognition to keep it before the people. This is always a good way to get people interested. It has been said that if you want something, praise it and people will respond to it. I know this is true because for years we have used this approach with success.

5. Sponsor a bus conference at your church. Some pastors feel that their church is not big enough to have a bus conference. Perhaps they say this because they want the conference for the wrong reason. We have a conference for the sake of our people, not just to get other churches to attend. In fact, the best way to start is to do it for your church. If other churches come, that is a plus, but do not make that the purpose.

There are many good men who could come to your church and be a blessing to your people regarding the bus ministry. You do not have to have a big-name speaker. Have someone who has a heart for and experience in the bus ministry. Do not make the members feel that the conference is for bus workers only. At first you may want to call it a Bus and Sunday School Conference or a Bus and Soul-Winning Conference. Make certain every member feels he is going to miss something important if he does not attend.

6. Preach about it occasionally. The heart of the people is greatly affected by the messages of the pastor. While you must be careful not to make any one thing an overly predominant topic, occasionally you should bring the bus ministry into your preaching. Let the people realize that it is not a whim or merely an optional ministry but rather a method to obey God's command to go into the highways and hedges reaching people for Christ.

7. Promote the positives of the bus ministry. Be careful in the pulpit not to discourage people inadvertently by telling them of things that happened that may have a negative connotation. People do not need to know of the problems that take place in any area of ministry unless they directly involve them. Promote the positives and deal with the problems. There is a price to pay to work in any ministry, and we should never deny that. People do not mind the sacrifice as long as they see the benefits and potential blessings.

8. Occasionally get the people involved churchwide. Coordination in this is very important. Whenever you have a big day in your church, you will probably have a greater need for extra workers in the bus ministry than in any other. Ask your people to jump in and help out. One good experience may cause a person to decide he wants to be a part of the blessings every week.

9. Accept what people *can* do and do not ask for more. Pastor, let people give what they can. If we are not careful we may expend more effort asking for more time than we do making the most of what time they are giving. Ministry is like a church budget. You cannot allot for more money than your people can give. Many pastors get into financial problems because they plan budgets based upon their hopes rather than the reality of what their people are giving. Before they know it, every service they are badgering their people for more money. The same can be true with the work of a ministry. Rather than building around what we have, we put ourselves in a desperation mode and begin to badger our people to give more time and effort. Eventually you will lose workers if you do this.

10. Invite others to visit with you. As a pastor I feel that taking other men and teenage boys soul winning and visiting with me is a very effective way of training them as well as building a relationship with them. Occasionally I will take a Saturday and give it to the bus ministry. I do what the other bus workers do. Whenever I do that, I want to take with me someone who is not in the bus ministry and let him experience the joy of working with these young people. This is a great idea for pastors trying to get more workers. If they see you do it and love it, they may decide to follow your example.

11. Exhibit pride in having a bus ministry in your church. Speak of your bus ministry with great pride and delight. Your people ought to believe that it just would not be the same without it. Again, if it is not a ministry you do with love and commitment, people will not respond.

12. Include it on your web page. Some people who are moving to your area are actually looking for a church with a bus ministry. You may even discover that someone who once worked in

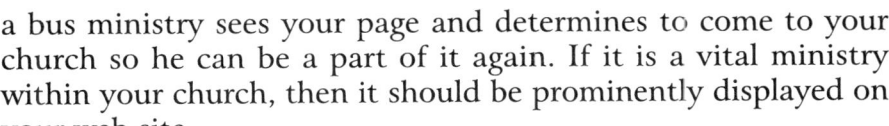

a bus ministry sees your page and determines to come to your church so he can be a part of it again. If it is a vital ministry within your church, then it should be prominently displayed on your web site.

13. Listen to your bus director. He may be struggling getting workers because he is not confident as to what he needs to do. He may need your help. Make certain that you are sensitive to the need for workers which he expresses. He wants to do a good job, but he may just need your help.

14. Don't stereotype. Who makes a good bus worker? Some pastors point their more blue-collar-type people towards the bus ministry while not even considering doctors, lawyers, business-men, or the more educated. That is a huge mistake. Pastor, there are people of all walks of life who make up our bus ministry. Do not rob anyone of the blessings that could be enjoyed in the bus ministry. The one you think would be least likely to get involved may be best suited to do so.

Pastor, you are ultimately responsible for making certain that you have enough servants to fill the opportunities and enough opportunities to allow everyone to serve. The bus ministry is an area that affords many places of service. You may be more ready for growth in your bus ministry than you realize. If you get busy recruiting, you may discover the pews are full of laborers just waiting for the opportunity to get to work.

Bus Director's Role in Getting More People Involved

IN THE previous chapter I taught what a pastor can do to enlist more bus workers. In this chapter I am going to give some tips to bus directors for doing the same. Some will be similar, but there are some distinct things a bus director can do to have plenty of workers for the routes at all times. It is not only the pastor's duty to recruit workers; the bus director must take an active role as well.

1. **Personally speak to people about joining the bus ministry.** Set up an appointment to meet with them in your office. Get them approved by the pastor before meeting with them. Here are some tips for that meeting.

♦ Share with them some positive information about the bus ministry.

♦ Tell them of the constant need for new workers.

♦ Tell them why you feel they may be a good fit for the bus ministry.

♦ Explain exactly what they would be doing.

♦ Tell them what the requirements are for workers.

♦ Ask them to pray about it and pray with them before they leave.

◆ Do not ask for an immediate answer.

◆ Make them feel comfortable turning you down. You have planted a seed that may produce at a later time.

2. Enlist and involve teenagers. More will be covered on this in another chapter, but suffice it to say here that teenagers make wonderful bus workers, and the bus ministry is a great way to help them grow as well.

3. Encourage families to get involved together. A good bus director will create a family-friendly environment.

◆ Be conscious of the families of your workers. Know their names. Send them birthday cards.

◆ Be thoughtful of the families. Let them know that you appreciate their sacrifice as well. Some spouses resent the bus ministry because they feel it keeps them apart from their spouses. You bring them together when you get the entire family involved.

◆ Publicly recognize the entire family when mentioning anything about that route. For example, instead of saying, "John Jones had eighty on his bus route this morning," say, "The John Jones family had eighty on their bus route this morning."

◆ Have events for bus workers that include the entire family.

◆ Recruit couples.

◆ Tell them of the blessings that working on a bus route could bring to their families.

◆ Have families who work together in the bus ministry give testimonies in the Sunday evening service.

4. Invite others to visit with you. This was mentioned to pastors, but I want to put a special emphasis on this to bus directors. Asking laymen in your church to visit with you accomplishes several things:

◆ Helps them to see the lives being affected.

◆ Gives you the chance to teach others to win souls.

◆ Builds relationships.

◆ May excite them actually to volunteer to work in the bus ministry.

◆ At the least it may cause them to pray for and give more to help the bus ministry.

5. Promote the positives of the bus ministry. Just as the pastor should do this, so should the bus director. Never tell the laypeople of your church what problems you are experiencing. Always speak of the blessings. The Bible speaks of a word fitly spoken. Just a positive word will sometimes plant the seed in another's mind that he too could be part of the bus ministry. A good bus director is a walking advertisement for workers.

6. Get the people involved churchwide from time to time. There may be special Sundays when the bus ministry is having a worker-intensive big day and may need extra workers to help. Enlisting members to help in some way on that day will often be the beginning of God's working on their hearts to enlist permanently. They may actually work on the bus or go out visiting. The more people who help, the more the blessings of the day are felt by many. Make certain you follow up with these people and thank them for their work.

7. Accept what people *can* do and do not ask for more. This is your ministry in the church, and that means that to you nothing is more important. That may not be true in their lives. They may only have so much to give. Accept it with gratitude and graciousness.

◆ Praise them for what they **do** without bringing up what they **do not do.**

◆ Watch out that you are not pushing them beyond their time constraints.

◆ Do not put people in uncomfortable positions.

◆ Make them want to do more by being grateful for what they are doing.

8. Deal with problems privately. Do not broadcast to the entire church some problem that took place on a bus route that morning. The people involved with solving problems are the only ones who need to know about them.

9. Ask workers to recruit others. This is a great method, and I will deal with it in more detail in another chapter.

10. Keep the pastor informed on your need for workers so that he can help you. Many bus directors get frustrated because the pastor does not know that they are struggling with too few workers. Communicate the needs to the pastor. Do not expect him to do all the work, but don't get into the mode of thinking you are in it all by yourself.

11. Do not badger people or attempt to shame them into joining the bus ministry. Once you have made the effort to enlist someone, do not constantly bring it up to him, or he may begin to avoid you. Rather than growing into the idea of working in the bus ministry, he may run from it because he may build up a resistance to your constant trying to make him feel guilty. A good recruiter makes people want to do something, not feel guilty because they won't.

12. Do NOT steal workers from other ministries. Good will is important for recruiting. The leaders of other ministries will support you if they have a good taste for the bus ministry. Few things will hinder this more than your taking their workers, as if their ministry is not as important as yours. Be considerate and even recommend some people to other ministry leaders. Not everyone is right for the bus ministry. Learn to accept that.

13. Introduce new bus workers with fanfare at your weekly bus meeting. When people join, make them feel special and do not let them just slip in, or they may just slip back out.

- Have them stand.
- Welcome them warmly.
- Tell everyone on which route they will be working.
- Tell a little about them.
- Have everyone applaud for them.
- Encourage everyone to shake hands with them after the meeting and personally welcome them.

Bus director, you must be aware that one of the most important duties of your job is to get the people you need. One thing you must remember is what Dr. Hyles used to say, "Don't use your people to build your ministry, but use your ministry to build your people." That applies to you and the bus ministry. Never look at workers as a commodity necessary to build and operate your ministry. Look at them as people who need an opportunity to serve the Lord and the guidance to do so effectively. Love them. Serve them. Minister to them. If you have the right attitude, you will never have a shortage of fellow laborers.

Involving Workers
in Recruiting

WHEN A COLLEGE is trying to recruit a young man to play football at their institution, they will often have another player or even an alumnus to help in the recruiting process. Most people are influenced by their peers far more than they are by the one in charge. Sure, you are going to say good things about the bus ministry; but if they want the real scoop, they are going to ask someone they know and trust who is already involved. Many great bus workers first volunteered because of the influence of others. If you get good at this, you will always have an abundance of good workers. The pastor and the bus director should be aware of this and do certain things that will encourage their present workers to recruit.

1. Make your workers aware of encouraging others to join. Most people recruit because they know the need for it. They are going to be focused on their route, not the entirety of the bus ministry, unless you make them aware of it. Keep it in front of them regularly so that they know how important they are to the process. Let them know specifically what the needs are.

2. Drop a name of someone they know well who you feel would be a good worker. Perhaps you are meeting with someone over whom they have some influence. Let them know and ask them to pray and put in a good word after you have met with the person. Teenagers are great at recruiting their friends. Encourage them to talk to other teens about getting involved.

3. Have them enlist others to help with a big day. When you know you will need extra workers to help with a big day, get the bus workers to help get the workers they need. That will get them in the mode of recruiting.

4. Solve their issues quickly and to their satisfaction. A happy bus worker is a good recruiter. If you address their concerns, they will feel good about recommending their friends and loved ones to join. If they feel you do not treat them with respect and consideration, they will not want their friends to join.

5. Point out the blessings in the midst of the difficulties. What you promote they will repeat. If a bus breaks down and you make it sound like a tragedy, your workers will describe the bus ministry as a difficult one. However, if you talk only about the good, your workers will see the good in every challenge, and that is what they will talk about. Your outlook determines others' attitudes, and their attitudes will determine the opinion of potential workers.

6. Have recruiting promotions. There may be times when you desperately need new workers. You may want to have a contest with your workers to see who can get a new worker and also to see who can get the most. It could even be a contest among the bus routes. See which route can recruit the most new workers. Remind them that they are not necessarily recruiting them for their own route. Contests are great ways to involve others in what you are trying to accomplish.

7. Recognize someone when he has recruited a new worker. Make a big deal out of it. Always recognize and praise what you want your workers to do. Do this privately as well as in public. That worker will want to do it again, and the other workers will see how important it is as well.

8. Send problems up and successes down. This is huge. If you want to get your workers talking about the difficult things in the bus ministry, then tell them all about those difficulties. If you want them to speak of the blessings and successes, then speak of those. When there are problems, take them to the pastor. When there are blessings, take them to your workers.

9. Ask them to pray for laborers. Jesus saw the multitudes and commanded that the disciples pray for laborers. I believe that it is the duty of every Christian to see the fields and pray that the Lord of the harvest would send forth more laborers into the harvest. When you pray in your meetings, pray for more workers. Your workers hear your prayers, and that will help them to do likewise.

10. **Involve bus parents.** This is used far too seldom, but it can be very effective. Once you reach the parents, perhaps the bus captain could ask them to help on the bus from time to time. They may just be there to help watch the kids or to help hand out materials, but think what this may do for them. Obviously, you must be careful that they represent the church properly, but what could be better than to make them feel they are needed? Perhaps the first time you ask them could be on a big day, but do not underestimate the potential of the parents.

11. **Teach your workers how to recruit workers.** Anything you want done you must teach. Do not assume they know how to go after workers. Give them pointers on how they can do so.

A great ministry is a self-perpetuating one. It ought to be the task of everyone; but if we do not understand that, we will be left with doing it by ourselves.

Involving Teens in
the Bus Ministry

IN THE search for the workers needed to operate our bus ministries, we should not overlook a resource that is often right in front of our eyes. Teenagers are a group within the church who are perfectly suited for the bus ministry and for whom the bus ministry can provide great opportunities and blessings. Some churches even build their youth group around the bus ministry.

As a young teenager, I began working on a bus route. By the time I was sixteen years old, I was a bus captain. In fact, as soon as I was old enough to drive and obtain my driver's license, I took the position of bus captain. It was life-molding for me and I believe can be for any teenager who works on a bus route. So many good things come about in the lives of the teens who work in the bus ministry.

- They learn to serve the Lord.
- They learn to serve people who are less fortunate.
- They learn to have compassion.
- They learn to win souls.
- They learn to work hard.
- They learn to work with children.
- They learn how to deal with adverse conditions.

- ◆ They learn to take responsibilities.
- ◆ They learn to be unselfish.
- ◆ They learn good skills for working with people.
- ◆ They stay busy doing good instead of getting into trouble.
- ◆ They learn the heartbeat of God and the church.

Churches are full of teenagers who are waiting to be challenged into service. In fact, one of the greatest untapped resources in most churches is the teens. We have a youth department with Sunday school and activities, but teenagers are eager to be more involved in the life of their church. Whether it is through teen soul winning, teen choirs or the bus ministry, they want to be used of God to see people saved as a result of their efforts. We treat teenagers like they are interested only in playing, when in truth they are often the most willing to serve and can add great energy and excitement to a bus route. We have many teens involved in our bus ministry. Here are some of the ways we get them involved.

1. Take a genuine interest in them. When a teenager recognizes that you are investing your time, effort and resources for him, he realizes you take teens seriously. Many others don't. Do not make them feel you are recruiting them just to use them. They need to feel they are valued, not just used. They cannot feel like they are a number or a hired hand. Teens will serve where they feel a sense of being valued.

- ◆ Show them your love, and they will share it with others.
- ◆ Show interest in them, and they will show interest in your bus kids.
- ◆ Value them, and they will value others.
- ◆ Invest in them, and they will invest in bus children.
- ◆ Help them, and they will help others.
- ◆ Give of yourself to them, and they will give of themselves to others.

Teens are ardent about reality. They hate phoniness. They seek out those who are genuine, and they had better find it in the work of God, or they will find it in the world.

2. Let them know they are needed. People often do not volunteer for a ministry because they feel that they are not needed. They get the idea that others are already doing all that needs to be done, and often they even feel they are inadequate to do the job. Present the need to your teens, and let them recognize they are not only wanted but needed on your route. Invite a teen to visit your route with you to see what it is like. Let them catch the burden by seeing it firsthand. Tell them stories about those on your route so they understand the need those kids have for someone to love them and care about them. A teenager with a burden is an almost unstoppable force.

3. **Invest time in training them.** Barnabas invested in Paul after his conversion. Paul invested in Timothy. In whose life are you making an investment? The Dead Sea is dead because it has no outlet to keep the waters flowing. A dead Christian is dead for much the same reason. He is taking in but has no outlet for the things he has learned. Do not merely recruit these young lives without investing time and training in them. It is a mistake to get a teenager to work on a route and feel he is being used to help the route without anyone's taking a special interest in him. The investment in the life of a teen is well worth it and will bring eternal rewards.

4. **Take the teens to conferences.** Youth conferences are great, and, in fact, we conduct a National Young Fundamentalist Conference every year; but many of us experienced our lives being influenced before there were all these youth conferences. We attended Bible conferences, bus conferences, Sword Conferences, and even pastors' conferences. Take your teens to hear good preaching. The more preaching of the Word of God they hear, the more likely they are to get involved serving the Lord. It was the preaching I heard as a teenager that helped me make major decisions in my life.

5. **Relate to them by learning to communicate with them.** It was because of my love for teens that I got involved with the newer methods of social networking. It was like learning a new language, but it was a language they understood and to which they related. Use the Internet to stay in touch with the teens. Use social media to communicate the bus ministry to them. I use Facebook, email, texting, and phone calls to stay in touch during

the week and to share what God is doing in the ministry. All of these are great with teens.

6. **Trust them with responsibility.** Give them a job to do, and let them do it and feel it is theirs. If they feel you cannot run the bus without their job being done, it will help them to be more faithful. They need to be trusted just like adults. Assign them to be in charge of going to the doors, taking attendance, leading the singing, teaching, running game time, or whatever needs to be done. Let them take ownership of that job. Supervise them but allow it to be their area of responsibility. Don't be afraid to let them have some of the responsibility. They can handle it and actually would love the opportunity. Responsible adults are those who learned to take responsibility as teenagers.

7. **Praise them and give them credit for doing a good job.** We must not encourage by correcting all the time. Praise is the greatest motivator of all. If they do the job, praise them even if it was not as good as or exactly the way you would have done it. Be quick to praise their efforts. Speak words of encouragement. Let them know you are proud of them and that they are doing a good job.

8. **Let the other teenagers see and hear how much fun it is to be a bus worker.** Do not tell them the bad or the horror stories. Make it look and sound fun. They should feel that the most exciting and fun ministry in the world is the bus ministry. Teens can put up with more inconveniences than adults without even noticing. Sell them on the fun, and they will willingly overcome all difficulties to fulfill their duties.

9. **Recognize and promote teenagers within the bus ministry.** That is what good companies do. Why do we bypass teenagers? If the best-qualified person is a teenager, then consider giving him the job. Many churches have used college students to be the leaders so much that the teens begin to resent them. If your teens feel that they are overlooked, they will feel they are second-class workers. Whenever you are seeking a new bus captain, let teenagers know you are considering them.

10. **Listen to their ideas.** Some of the best ideas come from fresh minds. Teens are creative. They can be helpful in coming up

with new programs, games, promotions, and many other things. Take their ideas seriously. Thank them for contributing their ideas even if you cannot use them. Never shoot down their ideas. Consider them and even help them to understand why it may not work and help them come up with alternative ideas. Encourage their creativity, and they will do wonders to help you grow.

I speak to pastors often who claim they do not have enough workers to expand their bus ministries. At the same time they have youth programs that are built around play and pleasure. How sad that they are creating two disservices by not seeing the potential of their teens. That is a mistake. Don't conduct a bus ministry just for the bus kids. Do it for the teenagers as well. Utilize, love and train the workers God has given you. There are teenagers in your church who are just waiting to be asked to help in the work. Find them, enlist them, train them, and see what great things God can do in and with their lives.

ORGANIZING WORKERS
FOR GROWTH

IN READING about the big events in the Bible where many people were saved, we discover that there were some organization and preparation made ahead of time. For example, it would have been impossible for the church on the day of Pentecost to handle three thousand baptisms and new additions to the church if there had not been some organization and preparation ahead of time.

Notice what the Bible says about Jesus and the seventy that He appointed in the work of getting out the Gospel and winning souls.

"After these things the Lord appointed other seventy also, and sent them two and two before his face into every city and place, whither he himself would come.

"Therefore said he unto them, The harvest truly is great, but the labourers are few: pray ye therefore the Lord of the harvest, that he would send forth labourers into his harvest."—Luke 10:1, 2.

Jesus obviously was making sure things were prepared for His arrival. First, it is clear that He knew He was going to those locations; second, He was expecting something big to happen. If we expect big things to happen, then we likewise must prepare. We are told that we should do things decently and in order.

An organized work begins with organizing leadership. The

pastor not only must know what his goal is and how he plans to accomplish it, but he must also share that goal and plan with the other leaders. In the bus ministry, that would be the bus captains who are designated to lead their bus workers in fulfilling the goal and plan established by the pastor and bus director. In the Sunday school, that would include the teachers and officers. In the church, it would include all the workers who are involved in the various aspects of the church.

For example, if you are planning for a big drive-in attendance, then you would want to make certain that those who park the cars are able to accommodate the volume of vehicles you are expecting. If you feel there will be many baptisms, then you must make certain you have all the necessary things to accommodate that. Planning ahead will avoid confusion and even prevent potential bad feelings. Many a big day was the result of a good intention, but bad planning created more damage than good.

The Bible is a Book of order. The work of the Lord must be done in an orderly fashion. We see it from the beginning in the Genesis account of Creation, in the organization of the laws and commandments; and the Bible ends with a foretelling of orderly events in the Book of Revelation. Even the judgments of the Lord were given in an order. However, so often the work of the local church is a "Let's just see what happens" kind of ministry. Here are some simple instructions for organizing your ministry leaders for production and growth.

1. Leadership must share the same passion for the work as the pastor. This passion does not just happen. In fact, staff and other leaders often become frustrated with the pastor because they do not "get the picture" or share the pastor's passion for the work. It is the pastor's job to convey what the passion and vision are so that the workers can have them in their own hearts.

It takes some time for passion to grow. Passion will not just "catch on" in one rousing speech or in one staff meeting. Passion in the workers comes as a result of your sharing your passion over and over and showing your commitment to the goal. Passion begins in your heart and then is passed on to another and then another. However, it must burn in your heart even if it burns alone for a while.

Many pastors are guilty of wanting everyone to share their vision just because they say so, rather than taking the time to develop that passion in their leaders and members. Many a special day was thwarted because the only one with the vision for the goal was the pastor. In frustration he scolds his people for something to which they were never committed. An unmotivated team is the fault of a presumptuous coach.

2. Know the strengths of your leaders. To get the most out of leadership, we must know the strengths **and** weaknesses of those who lead with us. In taking the time to learn their strengths, we can help them reach their potential. Likewise, if I take time to learn their weaknesses, I can either help strengthen them or work around them in those areas. There are some who make better workers than captains, and others who would be better bus drivers or teachers. Learn the strengths of your workers and lead them to the right area of ministry.

"And unto one he gave five talents, to another two, and to another one; to every man according to his several ability; and straightway took his journey."—Matt. 25:15.

One of the most disruptive mistakes bus directors and pastors make is placing people in areas of leadership where they are not capable of fulfilling the expectations. We try to force a square peg into a round hole and wonder why it doesn't work. We need to ask God for wisdom in this area of placement. It is important that we pay attention to whom we place as workers, as captains and as teachers.

If we see that we have poorly placed someone, we must not blame him for his lack of productivity. We must either better equip him or find an area better suited to him. By the way, if you want to discourage someone, allow him to flounder in a ministry in which he is destined to fail. Be careful that you place people in the best place and are quick to recognize if you did not.

3. Challenge the workers to continue growing and learning in their areas of service. All of us can and should continue to learn and grow in each area of our lives and responsibilities. We need to challenge our workers to do so as well. Pastors attend conferences and listen to other pastors to equip themselves better.

However, we often forget our fellow laborers who also need help and encouragement. Here are some ways you can help them.

Personally teach them. Spend time with them to let them know of ideas, promotions, songs, leadership skills, examples of other success stories, and ways that they can better lead and produce. Personal coaching is the best way to improve the skills of a member of your team.

Provide materials for them. Provide books, videos or audios that will help them with goal setting, overcoming failures, and working through obstacles and difficulties, or that will help them develop their leadership abilities. Be aware of what is available to help them and make it available to them at no cost.

Make it possible for them to attend meetings like preaching conferences and bus conferences that will instruct, strengthen and encourage them. The pastor is not the only one who needs refreshing in ministry.

4. Bus directors and pastors must help staff members to get along with one another. Growth creates more possibilities for issues. We are human and we do not always agree. Sometimes we even get selfish and want things our own way. Conflicts happen.

We see this when reading of the leadership of the Lord Jesus with His own disciples. They often disagreed with and misunderstood one another. They were often driven by their personal interests rather than the work at hand. However, the Lord Jesus spent time teaching and helping them to work together as a team.

The reason I placed this in this chapter is twofold. First, it is because I know that growth creates conflict. Second, the wise leader prepares for conflict before it happens. Many a conflict could have been avoided or at the very least been easily resolved had we been prepared. Many great works have been diminished because of divisions among workers. If you go to a football practice, you will often see fights erupt among teammates. That happens because in the heat of the work, tempers flare. I wish we were all spiritual enough never to get in the flesh, but in truth we are not.

Pastor, are you preparing for growth? If not, then do not be surprised if you are not growing. We know that God gives the increase. About that there is no debate. Here is the question: Does He give the increase to those who believe enough to be prepared or to those who never expect a thing? I think we know the answer to that question, so let's prepare ourselves for the blessings of God that come from our labors.

MAN BEHIND THE WHEEL, THE BUS DRIVER

H E IS THE captain of the ship. The safety of lives and the reputation of the church are a part of his responsibility. He can be taken for granted at times, yet without him we are shut down. His job is unlike any others within the ministry. He is that one who sits behind the steering wheel and drives our bus on Sunday mornings.

We know what his duty is. It is to drive the bus. We think we know his qualifications, but do we really? There are few people in the bus ministry upon whom we depend more than the ones who drive our buses. Because they are so vital to the ministry, I felt it would be negligent of me not to address what I see as the vital attributes we should seek in our bus drivers.

1. **Must have commercial license.** For those who may not know, let me tell you exactly what a **Commercial Driver's License (CDL)** is. This may be important for you to know and understand. **Never** allow anyone to drive your bus without this license.

A **Commercial Driver's License** (CDL) is a driver's license required in the United States to operate any type of vehicle which has a gross vehicle weight rating (GVWR) of 26,001 lb (11,793 kg) or more for commercial use, or transports quantities of hazardous materials that require warning placards under Department of Transportation regulations, or that is designed to transport 16 or more passengers, including the driver. This includes (but is not limited to) tow trucks, tractor trailers, and buses.

The Commercial Motor Vehicle Safety Act of 1986 was signed into law on October 27, 1986. The primary intent of the Act was to improve highway safety by ensuring that truck drivers and drivers of tractor trailers and buses are qualified to drive Commercial Motor Vehicles (CMVs), and to remove drivers that are unsafe and unqualified from the highways. The Act continued to give states the right to issue CDLs, but the federal government established minimum requirements that must be met when issuing a CDL.

Additional testing is required to obtain any of the following endorsements on the CDL. These can only be obtained after a CDL has been issued to the driver:

◆ P - Passenger Vehicle (Written and Driving Tests)

◆ S - School Bus (Written and Driving Test, Background Check, Sex Offender Registry Check and P endorsement)

2. Must be consecrated to the Lord. This position is not the one that may require the highest level of "standards." It is often a great starting place for one who wants to serve. However, please remember that you want a spiritual person driving your bus because of the very nature of what he is doing.

3. Must be committed to the ministry. When you enlist drivers into your bus ministry, you certainly want people who will be committed to their tasks. If you can't trust them to show up and do their jobs, then others are affected. They need to have the commitment to show up on time each week and fulfill their responsibilities.

4. Must have concentration. A good driver must not be distracted. That is one reason why the captain probably should not be the driver. The driver must be concentrating on the driving and the safety of the riders while the other workers are concentrating on the activities on the bus.

5. Must be careful and cautious. Obviously, not everyone who has a CDL license is as careful as he should be. Just drive down a busy highway and observe the truck drivers on the road. Negligence happens, so you need drivers who are cautious and who err on the side of safety. Do not assume they don't need occasional reminders, because we all do. Better to repeat the obvious than grieve the consequences of carelessness.

6. Must be calm and cool. Poise under duress is something a driver must possess. Buses get noisy when the kids are singing, cheering or playing games. A driver must be able not to get rattled by the kids or by other things that distract him.

7. Must be clean. As obvious as this may seem, I will state it anyway. The bus driver should be clean and bathed. You certainly do not want someone whose presence is offensive to others.

8. Must have command. With a bus driver's license comes a legal responsibility. The bus driver is a leader of sorts on that bus. This man has the lives of the riders as his responsibility. If there is something dangerous going on that could harm a rider, he must be willing to take the safety of the riders as his first priority. This may require him at times to insist on certain safety matters. He should be careful never to appear to be speaking against the captain; but in the instance of an immediate danger, he must also not be afraid to speak up.

9. Must be coachable. "Know it all's" need not apply for this responsibility. If a bus driver cannot take instruction, he should not be driving the bus. None of us know it all. All of us must submit to others who are in leadership. The bus driver must be humble to receive reminders of the things we can easily take for granted. Attending weekly meetings must not be beneath him. No matter how long we have done something, we must be willing to accept correction and reminders lest we become careless.

10. Must have compassion. The work of the bus ministry is about people. A bus driver's concentration is to get the children to Sunday school and church so that they can be saved and grow in their Christian lives. He must have a heart for that purpose which will make him more prayerful in his work for the Lord. Take him visiting with you. Let him see and know the way these kids live and the hurts they endure. Compassion makes a difference in every work we do for the Lord.

A final word to you who drive the bus: Please know how

important you are to every one of us who work in the bus ministry and, most importantly, to those children who ride your bus. You may at times feel that you are not as important as other workers. You are wrong. Your role is of the utmost importance. We appreciate you. Only eternity will tell of the rewards that await you for being there early to get the bus ready and for week after week doing your job.

SHOULD I BE A
BUS WORKER?

*(Written for someone who may be contemplating
getting involved in the bus ministry)*

YOU MAY have been approached by someone and asked if you would be interested or willing to help out on a bus route. Perhaps you saw an announcement in the bulletin or heard an announcement from the pulpit that there is a need for new workers in the bus ministry. Whatever the cause, you are wondering if maybe this is a place where you should volunteer to serve the Lord; but you are just not sure. Sometimes a person wonders if he is the right person to be a bus worker, so I decided that I would write something just for you.

Joining the bus ministry is an important decision. I truly believe that almost anyone could work in some capacity in the bus ministry, but that does not mean that everyone should. This decision is an important one, because young lives are at stake. The last thing these kids need is a revolving door of workers coming in and out of their lives. They need the consistency of people who are really investing themselves into their lives. To assist you with your decision, here are a few questions to ask yourself.

1. Do you have a godly love for children? Most people love kids, but for some there is a deep desire to be a blessing and a help to them. They have a burden for young people and want to make a difference in their lives. This is a good sign the bus ministry may be a good fit for them. Kids need people who care for them spiritually. It cannot be a mere assignment. They must sense the care and desire within us that we want to be with them and help them.

2. Are you seeking a way you can serve the Lord? I meet so many Christians who have been on the sidelines for so long, and they are ready to get into the action of doing something for the Lord. The bus ministry is a terrific place for many who want to serve the Lord but don't know where to begin.

3. Do you love winning souls, or would you like to learn how to win souls? Over the years I have discovered that people who want to reach as many people as possible for Christ find their opportunity to do so in the bus ministry. Without a doubt, the bus ministry is one of the most fruitful places a person can serve Christ.

4. Are you available to visit on Saturday mornings and ride the bus on Sundays? Availability is important because this is a ministry that requires the consistent commitment of time. Can you invest time on Saturday mornings to visit the route as well as be available on Sundays to ride the bus to pick up the children and take them back home? It may be that Saturdays are not available for now. Perhaps there is still something you could do to help on a route on Sundays, such as drive or be an extra helper on the bus.

5. Are you trustworthy? Simply put, the bus ministry is not the right fit for someone who cannot be counted on to do his duty. There are too many people who would be counting on you each week; and if you cannot be counted on, it probably is not right for you.

6. Are you teachable? Please know that there is very little you need to know to start working on a bus route. If you are someone who is willing to learn, you are perfect. The bus ministry does not require specific skills or abilities, but it does require that its workers have humble hearts. They must do what they are asked to do and not be afraid to take instruction.

7. Has the Lord been burdening your heart? People will tell me that every time they hear about the bus ministry, they wonder if they should get involved. Maybe God is speaking to your heart about it. Maybe He is putting a burden on your heart. A burden is often a very still small voice within that tells us to get involved and do something.

8. Do you have something to offer that is needed? If someone has a need for a specific thing and you have the exact thing he needs and can offer it to him, perhaps you should do so. For example, the call goes out that there is a need for a driver with a Commercial Driver's License to drive a Sunday school bus, and you happen to have one. Well, then, there is your opportunity. You have it and there is a need for it. Often we miss the obvious by not recognizing a need that we could and probably should fill.

9. Have you been praying about it? If not, do so, fervently. I am not saying you should pray as to whether or not you should serve God. That is not something about which we need to ask. However, we certainly should ask God to lead us to the right places to serve. Make it a matter of serious prayer if you have any thought that maybe you should volunteer.

10. Have you ever volunteered to help one Sunday on a route? If you want to know what being a part of a bus route is like and whether or not you would be able and want to do it, perhaps being a helper on a bus when there is a need would give you a firsthand way of finding out if it is for you. Maybe you could visit on a bus route some Saturday and ride the bus the next day. Put your toes in the water, and you may decide to launch on out into the deep.

11. Have you sought counsel from the pastor or some other of your spiritual leaders? When in doubt, get advice. When you are not sure, don't be afraid to ask. The ones who lead you will most certainly tell you whether or not they think it would be the best place for you to serve.

12. Are you able? As obvious as it seems, do not neglect to know whether or not you are able to do what needs to be done. In other words, count the cost. Some people have health issues that may prevent them, although some of the greatest bus workers have been handicapped people. Make sure you have the ability to do what needs to be done; if not, God will lead you to another ministry where you can serve.

We always need bus workers. However, we need the right people to become bus workers. Consider it thoughtfully and prayerfully. It will be a great blessing but only if it is where God wants you to be.

TRAINING A NEW BUS WORKER

TRAINING a new worker is one of the greatest opportunities and responsibilities a bus captain has because it means he is helping new laborers to reach the harvest of souls. It is important to accept the challenge of helping teach others to do something for Christ. It is easy to assume that everyone will know what he should do, but that is not the case. He needs help, and you must consider it part of your responsibility as a bus captain to train your workers properly and thoroughly.

The following is a checklist for you to use as you begin training your new workers. These are the areas that you have to cover in order to help them become successful bus workers. Every moment that you spend training them is critical. Before I give you the checklist, let me give you three responsibilities that you have with all the workers you train on the bus route.

1. **Encourage them.** Many people are nervous when they begin working on a bus route. All of us feel inadequate when we start a new venture. Encourage your new workers to feel that they can do it and to keep on going even when they are struggling. Be patient and positive for them through their learning mistakes. Praise their good while gently correcting their errors.

2. **Make them accountable.** Everyone needs accountability. Check with them every week to be sure that they are present for the bus meeting and that they are prepared for Sunday. Give

them homework and prepared assignments and make certain you follow up with them on these.

3. Set a good example. Be the kind of worker that you want to train. Show them how it is done. Let them see your faithfulness. Let them see your fears, but let them see your willingness to overcome your fears. Let them know the obstacles that you have overcome, but by all means be a good example to them.

Now let's talk about what you are trying to accomplish to help them become good bus workers. The following is a list of things that you will want to instill in your new workers. Some of these are assignments, and some of them are things you need to teach them how to do.

1. Help them develop a burden for the souls of the children. A burden for souls is not automatic. It is something you need to help instill in them. Share your burden and let them know the importance of caring for and loving the kids.

2. Talk to them about the importance of faithfulness. Scheduling our priorities is the only way that we will be successful in the areas of our lives. Make certain they know what is expected of them and when. Make faithfulness of utmost importance in their minds.

3. Talk to them about their appearance. Don't assume they know how to dress properly on the bus. The best way to encourage them is for you to dress properly and tell them why. This is so that they know how important it is to look right when they are out visiting and on the bus on Sunday.

4. Teach them how to make a successful visit. Visiting the route is essential. Make certain that even if they are going with you, you are teaching them the entire time you are visiting. Between visits point out what you are doing and why. Do not assume they will just pick it up and understand without your telling them. Here is a list of things to teach about visitation.

♦ How to approach doors. This initial approach is something that they need to understand and know. Teach them how to go to the door, how to knock on the door and wait for the person to answer the door.

◆ How to greet people by telling them who they are, from where they have come, and by extending an invitation to them to ride the bus

◆ How to carry on a conversation at the door. The initial conversation is very important to try to win the child and his parents to yourself in order to be able to get them to church.

◆ How to promote a big day

◆ How to invite people to church

◆ How to get the parents' permission

◆ How to find new children

5. Make certain they know how to lead a person to Christ. A bus worker should also be a good soul winner. The bus route is a good place to train soul winners. Be thorough in doing so. Spend some time just trying to win souls so you can teach them how to do it.

◆ Teach them the Romans Road. It is very vital that you teach them exactly how to present the Romans Road to the person that they are trying to win.

◆ Help them mark their New Testaments. Be sure that they have good soul-winning New Testaments; then help them mark them so that they can use them effectively.

◆ Teach them how to lead a person to trust Christ.

◆ Teach them how to lead a person to receive Christ into his heart.

◆ Teach them how to give a person assurance of his salvation.

◆ Teach them how to get a person to come to church the following Sunday and to walk the aisle.

◆ Teach them how to get their converts baptized.

◆ Have them read *Let's Go Soul Winning* by Dr. Jack Hyles several times while you are training them.

6. Teach them how to deal with certain situations they will face. Prepare them for the things that you know can happen on the bus.

◆ Bad behavior

◆ A child getting hurt or sick on the bus

◆ A child that gets scared

◆ Bullying

7. **Teach them the importance of prayer.** Encourage them to pray throughout the week for their work as well as for the riders. Pray with them and then encourage them to pray daily.

8. **Teach them how to do the program on the bus.** Make certain not to throw them into a situation where they have not been trained. Perhaps you could give them a small part at first and practice with them on Saturday so they feel confident Sunday morning.

9. **Teach them the importance of having a good spirit and keeping a good attitude.**

10. **Work with them on skills they may not have learned before.** For some people, no one has ever taken the time to teach them. This is your opportunity to invest in them. Take the time to teach them some things that may seem second nature to you but that they may have never learned.

◆ People skills

◆ Leadership skills

◆ Activity skills

◆ Conversational skills

A *good* bus captain is one who works well with the kids on the bus route. A great bus captain is one who does the same but who also reproduces himself by training others also to work well with the bus kids. Your influence for Christ is multiplied when you take the time to train others. Think of it this way: The people who come to church and get saved on your route will be part of your reward in Heaven, but potentially many more will be saved as a result of their witness and as a result of the witness of the other bus workers whom you train. Eternity alone will reveal all in whose salvation you played a part.

A BUS WORKER'S
WALK WITH GOD

OVER THE years I have been blessed to work with scores of good people in the bus ministry. Many of them have continued to serve for decades without losing their love and passion for their routes. Others, however, have come and gone. They are good people, but for some reason they got tired or lost their passion for the ministry. In some cases they have fallen away from the Lord and have quit not only the bus ministry but also the church altogether. In this chapter I am going to put my finger on the one thing a bus worker must maintain to remain faithful.

There is a temptation to those who serve the Lord to become lax in their own personal relationship with the Lord. We get so busy doing the work that we fail to be prepared for the work. We start going through the motions rather than fulfilling the duty of love. When it comes to our work for the Lord, it is a priority to maintain a daily and personal walk with Him. Those who lose their passion for the work are those who first lost their commitment to that walk.

Much of what is in this book will deal with the practical side of the bus ministry, such as organization, preparation, the bus ride, the program on the bus, the "how to's," and the important details. While all of these are very important, the most important aspect of our lives is our walk with God.

What may appear to be the obvious can easily become the

neglected. We are engaged in spiritual warfare, and there is no ministry where this is more evident than in the neighborhoods where we operate many of our routes. As we go into the highways and hedges, we enter spiritual warfare in our attempt, as Jude says, to pull them out of the fire. Satan battles mightily to keep the lost in darkness and sin. He fights the soul winner and bus worker in every way imaginable in an attempt to prevent them from reaching boys and girls with the Gospel of Jesus Christ.

Nursing home ministries have their own unique challenges, but I have never seen the satanic attacks there that I have seen in the bus ministry. The Devil is evidently much less concerned with our winning a person to Christ whose life is almost over than he is with our getting a young person who has a lifetime to serve Christ. The attacks of Satan on bus workers eclipse his assaults on the workers of any other ministry I have ever observed. Bus workers face daunting challenges that could dissuade and discourage them.

Having said that, I state that it is vitally important that those in any ministry, but especially the bus ministry, faithfully maintain a daily and personal walk with the Lord. We need to stay spiritually nourished and to have the fire of the Holy Spirit's power rekindled in our lives daily. There are simple but vital things that bus workers must do to remain diligent in their work for the Lord.

1. Spend time daily in the Bible. Jeremiah had a work God had called him to do. It was a difficult work. In fact, it was a work that few would or could sustain for very long. Jeremiah did what God had instructed him to do. He preached, he warned, and he proclaimed God's Word to the people, yet Jeremiah had no converts. He was not loved or appreciated and in fact was in the deepest dungeon of the prison. Jeremiah was discouraged and no longer wanted to continue. He became a bit angry with God and spoke sternly to Him.

> "O LORD, thou hast deceived me, and I was deceived: thou art stronger than I, and hast prevailed: I am in derision daily, every one mocketh me."

> "Then I said, I will not make mention of him, nor speak any

more in his name."—Jer. 20:7, 9.

Things were not going the way Jeremiah expected or planned, so he quit. He told God he would no longer preach. Jeremiah did what so many servants of God do. He gave up in frustration.

Then something wonderful happened. God's Word did its work in Jeremiah's heart. "But his word was in mine heart as a burning fire shut up in my bones, and I was weary with forbearing, and I could not stay" (vs. 9)

1. The Word was in his heart.

2. The fire of God was burning in his bones.

3. He quit fighting his call.

4. He reenlisted.

"Thy word have I hid in mine heart, that I might not sin against thee" (Ps. 119:11).

When the Word of God is hidden so deeply in your heart that it is sealed in your bones, then it will overwhelm your desire to quit. You **will** get discouraged, just as Jeremiah did. Resistance will come. Disillusionment will rear its head. Attacks will be launched at you. You need God's Word to permeate your heart so that when the temptation to discouragement comes, you will stay faithful. Bus worker, read your Bible. Do it every day. Be faithful to the Word, and you will remain faithful to the work.

2. Listen to teaching and preaching. When you arrive at church and the children have been delivered to their classes, what do you do? Do not become a mere spectator in the activities of Sunday school and church. God has ordained preaching to keep our hearts stirred, to instruct us in the way, and to give us the strength to fight through the challenges of ministry. I have known of churches where the bus workers hung out together drinking coffee and eating donuts during church. *After all,* they wrongly think, *we got up early and have been working for the Lord. We deserve a few minutes to relax, right?* Wrong. They need to get into a Sunday school class, and they need to be in church listening to the message. Bus workers should attend every church service. Even if you work in children's church, it is important to hear the preaching. Preaching will keep your heart stirred for winning souls and working to reach boys and girls for the Lord. Here are a few important suggestions.

◆ Be a member of a Sunday school class even if you teach a children's class. You need the fellowship and accountability.

◆ Be in church to hear the preaching unless you are working in a children's church.

◆ Be in church every Sunday and Wednesday night.

◆ During the week, listen to preaching every chance you get.

3. Stay fervent in prayer. Prayer is vital for the Christian soldier. Prayer is connecting with Heaven's throne of grace. This is where we find grace to help in the time of need. This is where we get our hearts and minds clean and clear from sin. Oh, listen to me, Christian soldier: spend time with God in prayer.

◆ Pray for wisdom. "If any of you lack wisdom, let him ask of God, that giveth to all men liberally, and upbraideth not; and it shall be given him" (Jas. 1:5).

◆ Pray for more workers. "Pray ye therefore the Lord of the harvest, that he will send forth labourers into his harvest" (Matt. 9:38).

◆ Pray for those on your bus route and their families to be saved. "Brethren, my heart's desire and prayer to God for Israel is, that they might be saved" (Rom. 10:1).

◆ Pray for the spiritual growth of your bus riders.

"And this I pray, that your love may abound yet more and more in knowledge and in all judgment;

"That ye may approve things that are excellent; that ye may be sincere and without offence till the day of Christ.

"Being filled with the fruits of righteousness, which are by Jesus Christ, unto the glory and praise of God."—Phil. 1:9–11.

◆ Pray for victory over sin. "Deliver us from evil"(Matt. 6:13).

◆ Pray for the power of the Holy Spirit. "If ye then, being evil, know how to give good gifts unto your children: how much more shall your heavenly Father give the Holy Spirit to them that ask him?" (Luke 11:13).

I have seen very few workers quit who had a faithful prayer life. "And he spake a parable unto them to this end, that men ought always to pray, and not to faint" (Luke 18:1). This verse preceded an entire passage that told the parable of a woman who kept on praying. Prevailing prayer is a deterrent to failure. As long as you keep your prayer life right, you will stay busy for the Lord. Pray, bus worker; pray.

Do not be a casualty. Do not forfeit the blessings of God. Do not become weary and sacrifice the lives of precious children who need you. You are important, but your walk with God is vital if you are to remain committed to your cause and God's purpose.

IS IT A JOB OR
A CALLING?

"And I thank Christ Jesus our Lord, who hath enabled me, for that he counted me faithful, putting me into the ministry;

"Who was before a blasphemer, and a persecutor, and injurious: but I obtained mercy, because I did it ignorantly in unbelief.

"And the grace of our Lord was exceeding abundant with faith and love which is in Christ Jesus."—I Tim. 1:12–14.

WEEKEND after weekend you work hard running your route. When Sunday is over you are more exhausted than most. You arrive late for Sunday lunch. Your afternoon nap is short if you get one at all. You carry not just the persons of children to church every Sunday: you carry their burdens and eternal souls deep within your heart.

In the winter when the weather is cold, you freeze as you go to each door to fetch the children. Your feet get wet, and your clothing gets dirty. You deal with snotty noses, the cries of a scared child, and sometimes the vomit of one who decided he couldn't hold down his breakfast any longer. You are a bus worker, and yours is not always an easy task.

So, bus worker, exactly why **are** you doing what you do? Is it something you merely volunteered to do; were you drafted to work on a route; or did the Holy Spirit of God impress upon your heart the burden to reach out to boys and girls in your area with the Gospel of Jesus Christ? I guess what I am asking you is this: Did God call you into the bus ministry, or is it just a job for you?

Let's face it: many people start in a ministry and last for awhile and then stop. I appreciate the work they did and the service they provided; but if it had been a calling, they would not have stopped. Some feel they have paid their dues or put in their time. Others feel called to become a part of another ministry, and that is certainly understandable. Sadly, some get disgruntled with something and quit serving God altogether, eventually even leaving church.

However, there are those people who stay with it year after year with faithfulness and diligence. What sets these people apart? I believe there are many people who feel a special call of God to be a bus worker. It has been my privilege to know many people who after 10, 20, 30 or even 40 years still faithfully serve as bus workers. They are a special type of people. To them there is seldom a thought of quitting. Oh, they have had their moments when Satan tried to discourage them, but they overcame the temptation to quit. They stayed with it.

In this chapter I want to address those of you who feel called to the bus ministry just as I feel called to pastor. Believe it or not, all of us have moments of doubt. We may feel inadequate. We may sense we are getting stale. Possibly even some discouragement has set into our lives. It happens to every servant of God. Allow me to do a little preventive maintenance that hopefully will get you through those times. When you are tempted to be discouraged, remember a few important things.

1. **The calling of God is a privilege.** Once on a Delta flight I was seated next to a fifty-year-old military man. One of the flight crew spoke over the PA system and recognized his service for our country. Everyone on the airplane applauded him. I spoke with him and was impressed with what he told me. He spoke of the honor of wearing the uniform and serving his country and that he wanted to serve as long as they would allow him. He saw it as more than his duty to serve. He saw it as his privilege.

It is even more of a privilege to wear the uniform of a servant of God. Bus worker, wear that calling with pride and joy. You are serving the Lord doing exactly what is called honorable in the Bible. Much is said in the Bible about the importance of children. Never feel that what you do is less than any other service to the Lord. The disciples who rebuked the people who were bringing children to Jesus so they could touch Him were in turn rebuked by Jesus. Your calling is sacred. Consider it an honor to serve God in this capacity.

2. The calling of God is a responsibility. It cannot be taken lightly that we have a responsibility to those to whom we minister and an even greater responsibility to the One whom we serve. Sometimes we may not feel like doing what we do for the sake of those kids. What should we do when we don't want to do what we are supposed to do?

"And whatsoever ye do, do it heartily, as to the Lord, and not unto men" (Col. 3:23).

Well, that pretty much sums it up. It is never enough to do it primarily for the children. Everything we do should first and foremost be "as to the Lord." People who are called to do something must never forget that their responsibility is to Him.

3. The calling of God is eternal. What do I mean by this? When God calls a person to do an eternal work, he must not expect his earthly rewards to match his effort. He must focus on the fact that eternity reveals the good he has done.

◆ From an earthly perspective, you make too many sacrifices; but from a heavenly one, you will have made too few.

◆ From an earthly perspective, you will have been overworked; but from a heavenly one, you will have worked far too little.

◆ From an earthly perspective, you receive far too little attention; but from a heavenly one, you will have received far too much acclaim.

Your spirit and attitude will depend upon the perspective from which you view your work. We pastors often feel sorry for ourselves on earth, but in Heaven we will be sorry for the earthly attitude we had of feeling sorry for ourselves. We are called, and we must know that the rewards we will receive are eternal rewards. Volunteers want instant acclaim or gratitude. Called people must not fall into that trap. Our results and our rewards cannot be measured by earthly measures. What we do is eternal and will be measured only in eternity.

So let me return to the question I asked at the very beginning of this chapter. Why are you doing what you do? Are you called? If so, please remind yourself regularly of these important principles lest ye faint. "Knowing that of the Lord ye shall receive the reward of the inheritance: for ye serve the Lord Christ"(Col. 3:24).

Worker, Don't Quit!

No work is more challenging, and none requires more faithfulness and commitment than that of the bus ministry; however, no work is more rewarding when it comes to winning souls and changing lives. Due to the level of commitment required and the ever increasing pressures of our daily lives, many workers are often tempted to quit. Worker, you cannot quit. You dare not quit, because the stakes are far too high. That said, sometimes we need to be reminded why our work is so important, and hopefully that will encourage us at those times when we feel like quitting.

1. **You may be the *only hope* for the children on your bus route.** There was a day when even our public schools would read and teach the Bible. They told the stories of Adam and Eve and spoke of sin and were not ashamed to speak of Jesus. That day is gone. Today holidays like Easter are being changed from celebrating the resurrection of Jesus to a celebration of bunnies and egg hunts. There was a day when most children lived in a home that believed in the Lord Jesus Christ. Today TV has so influenced the home that many children never hear the gospel story.

Just think—if you quit—who will take the Gospel to the children on your bus route? *Who?* By the way, you may be the only hope for their parents as well.

2. ***Hell* is a real place, and those who die without Christ will spend eternity there.** We cannot allow these children to die without Christ. When you read the story of Luke 16, you find that

the rich man is still in the torments of Hell. Is that what we want to let happen to the children on our bus routes? Who will tell the little ones about Jesus when they reach the age of accountability? There will be Saturdays and Sundays when you will wonder why you are working in the bus ministry, and that is when you must remind yourself that you are doing it because there is a real Hell.

3. Our lives are best lived and our time is best spent in the service of Jesus. There is not a more productive soul-winning ministry than the bus ministry. When you spend three to four hours visiting on Saturday and two or three hours on the bus on Sunday, you are making an eternal difference in the lives of young people.

There are many social and community activities in which you could be involved, but none that reach young people for Christ like the bus ministry does. One day you will realize that you did not merely spend your time working on that bus route: you invested time into something that will pay in eternal benefits. Not only is that true, but also it is true that the joy you experience now is worth the time invested in the life of a child or teenager on the route.

4. God called you to the bus ministry. If that is true, then did He call you to quit? Of course not. God has called each and every one of His children to reach others with the Gospel. We have to remember that we are not only in the bus ministry to fulfill a commitment, but we are in the bus ministry because God called us to serve Him. The Bible tells us not to grow weary in well doing. God would not have said that if He had not known that there would be times when we would get weary, but He did not call us to quit. He called us to finish. Some of the greatest blessings will come after one has been a faithful bus worker for a long period of time.

5. You encourage others to stay in the bus ministry. Your fellow workers are watching you. Someone may quit because you do, and that may lead him on a downward spiral. You may go on in another ministry, but he may not. It could be that you are the inspiration that keeps him going even when he feels like quitting.

Nothing we do is alone. When we sin, it affects someone. When we do right, it affects someone. When we quit, it affects someone. When we stay faithful, it affects someone. Think of that when you feel like giving up.

6. You encourage others by your faithful work. This is true not only in your church and ministry, but you may encourage others across America who hear, read or know about your work. We never know who may be blessed by our faithfulness. Your faithfulness in the bus ministry encourages others to stay faithful in their ministries. You never know who else might quit if they see you quitting your bus route. The relationships you form with other workers often strengthen until they become like family to you.

Someone is watching you, and you may be the reason he continues to serve in the bus ministry. Others may be inspired to give because of your faithfulness. A church member may be inspired to be faithful in attendance because of you. Even your pastor may find great encouragement by knowing that you are faithful. We do not realize the implications of an example of something as simple as faithfulness, but being an example in faithfulness is one reason we must keep going.

7. The bus ministry will keep you busy for the Lord. Let's face it—we are all lazy to a degree. Every Christian needs some ministry that allows him to serve the Lord. You have heard the statement "An idle mind is the Devil's workshop." The bus ministry will keep you busy serving the Lord. There is always something you can do to keep you busy when you are a bus worker. It also will keep you praying, and you can pray for your bus route anywhere. Stay busy for the Lord, bus worker. Don't quit.

8. Serving in the bus ministry will make you a better Christian. When I think of a great Christian, I think of one who reads his Bible daily, prays faithfully, attends church regularly, tells others about Jesus consistently, and lives his life as an example to others. These things are often required of us by merely serving as bus workers. Consider:

◆ Knowing that you are going to teach a class, give a short challenge on the bus, or even give a small lesson in the form of a puppet show will force you to read your Bible and study.

◆ Visiting those on your bus route and seeing the condition in which some of the children live and hearing stories of their circumstances will drive you to your knees in prayer.

◆ The bus ministry will encourage you to stay faithful to church. Your responsibility will make you think twice about staying home even when you don't feel well.

◆ The bus ministry gives you weekly opportunities to tell someone about Jesus. A bus worker is a laborer in the fields that are white unto harvest.

Participating in the bus ministry will give you opportunities to develop the characteristics of a good Christian.

9. You encourage your bus riders every time you visit them. We do not really know what is in the heart of a child often until he is an adult and finally shares his heart and feelings. Children often act brave when really they are filled with fear, hatred or anger. Often they look forward to your visit and wait all week for Sunday when they can attend Sunday school and church. You give them hope! The day you quit may be the day the Devil takes away the hope that child has. You may not ever know it until eternity.

10. You keep the fire alive in your church. I have felt the excitement in churches where there is a vibrant bus ministry, and I have sensed the excitement fading when they pull out of the bus ministry. There is no comparison in the two atmospheres. Bus worker, you are important. What you do keeps the fires burning in your church, allowing God to do a greater work.

If we could see into eternity to know the results and rewards awaiting us for our faithfulness, none of us would dare walk away from this great ministry. Is it tough at times? Do we often feel we are working in obscurity? Are there other ministries where we could coast a bit more? The answer is yes to all of these. However, never forget these reasons why you are important and needed; and perhaps when you are faced with the temptation to quit, you will tell yourself, "Don't quit!"

PATIENCE, A NECESSARY QUALITY FOR BUS WORKERS

PATIENCE is the mind-set as well as the attitude of a farmer or husbandman. He plants or sows seeds in the spring. He works and toils patiently through the growing season, dealing with whatever difficulty comes his way so that he can produce a harvest in the fall. There are many potential hardships that he may encounter. He may have to deal with a summer of intense heat or perhaps a drought. He may be forced to deal with flooding. A disease may spread which harms his crops, or animals may ravage them. However, no matter what hardships come his way, he does not quit. Instead, he works through them until he gathers the harvest in the fall. This defines patience.

"Flee also youthful lusts: but follow righteousness, faith, charity, peace, with them that call on the Lord out of a pure heart.

"But foolish and unlearned questions avoid, knowing that they do gender strifes.

"And the servant of the Lord must not strive; but be gentle unto all men, apt to teach, patient."—II Tim. 2:22–24.

Paul instructed Timothy to produce followers or disciples of the Lord. He admonished him not only to do this personally but to lead others to do so as well. Just as the farmer has patience and works through the difficulties of bringing a field from seed to harvest, so must we have patience in our work of bringing young people from where they are to a life of serving the Lord Jesus.

For our churches, we often desire to find people who have already been saved, baptized and trained to serve the Lord. We get the fruit and results from another worker in the field rather than go through the process and work of winning people to Christ, getting them baptized, and taking the time to train and disciple them in the work of the Lord. I am always thankful when the Lord sends workers our way, but our emphasis must be that of the Great Commission—not getting others' laborers to begin working our field. We are commanded to build soul-winning churches. In so doing we will have to learn to have the patience of the husbandman in several ways.

1. Sometimes we must patiently wait for their salvation. Not everyone we bring will get saved immediately. There will be plenty of seeds sown on your bus route which will not bring forth immediate fruit. Are you willing to continue to water? Are you willing to keep going back and showing them the love of Christ with your actions? Many of the ones who are most difficult to win become some of the greatest trophies of God's grace.

2. We must be patient in their spiritual growth. We are to win the lost and bring them to a place of service for the Lord. To do this we must have great patience with our converts. Growing a Christian is a laborious task. These children have no Christian influence in their lives six days a week. Nurturing them takes time. Satan has such a hold on so many people that we must literally, as Jude says, pull some out of the fire. Do not expect them to be mature Christians overnight. Expect a process and enjoy it.

3. We must be patient in developing their character. This is difficult because many of the children reached in the bus ministry have never been taught how to behave. In today's culture, character is seldom taught and rarely required. There is very little moral virtue. The children's manners are poor. Their obedience is spotty at best. They have not been trained in character. Be patient with them. Rejoice in every sign of progress.

One of the greatest keys to success in the bus ministry is

learning to be patient with those who do not behave. We must teach our workers that there will be kids who are going to lack training on how to behave. In fact, they may come from homes where no one even cares. It may be that the only attention they ever get is that which comes when they are misbehaving; therefore, misbehavior is the only way they know for getting attention.

A good worker will pray hard for God to give him the patience to endure the mischief that these kids may inflict upon him. He must be able to recognize the difference between mischief and meanness. Often we think a child is a bad child when in truth he is just seeking love and testing a worker to see if he will endure.

Many times it is that one who causes the most trouble who eventually becomes most used of God. I have never known an effective bus worker who was not patient. Just as Paul admonished Timothy to have patience, so must we admonish those who work with the bus children to have patience with those entrusted to them.

4. We must be patient in their failures. Worker, your bus kids will quit, make mistakes, fall into sin, and let you down. Do not give up on them. They are your responsibility. Love them through their worst failures. You never know when God will get hold of their hearts again; and if we are still loving them, we can see their lives brought back to God. Some may come back to God even after they are grown and have families of their own. Be patient with them.

Many years ago a godly Christian lady in Puerto Rico would go to the little neighborhoods where children lived and gather them up to walk with her to Sunday school and church. They had no bus or van, so they just walked the boys and girls to church every Saturday and Sunday. One little boy that walked with her every week was Rolando.

Rolando was one of those little boys who are a bit unruly, and he often ended up in a special class for children who could not behave. Even on the walk to the church Rolando would throw rocks or run off from the rest of the group. He was just one of "those kids." We have all had them.

In spite of the trouble he caused week after week, the faithful Christian lady would go by each week, tell the boys and girls of

Jesus' love, and gather them up to walk with her to church.

Over twenty years passed, and Rolando left Puerto Rico and moved to America. He got married and had two boys of his own. He got a good job and began living the American dream.

One Saturday morning two young ladies knocked on his door and told him that they were inviting boys and girls to ride a bus to Sunday school. Rolando's mind went back to the lady who would come by his house when he was a boy and walk him to Sunday school. Rolando gave permission for his two boys to ride the bus to Sunday school.

After two weeks he and his wife decided to attend and went with them. Within a month the whole family had trusted Christ as Saviour. Today Rolando is serving the Lord as a soul winner and bus driver all because of a lady who week after week loved him enough to be patient with him and his mischief and walk him to church.

There are literally thousands and thousands of boys and girls in our towns today that need someone patiently to share with them the love of the Lord Jesus. We must be patient with their spiritual growth, personal behavior and development of Christian character. We don't know what is going to happen to them in the future, so we need to be busy reaching everyone we can with the Gospel. We must be patient because we do not know who will eventually become a servant of the Lord like Rolando.

Although Rolando does not know what happened to the other boys and girls that walked to Sunday school with him some thirty-five years ago, he does remember the godly lady coming by each week, telling him of God's love for him, and planting the seed of the Gospel in his heart.

AVOIDING AND OVERCOMING DISCOURAGEMENT

"Then I said, I will not make mention of him, nor speak any more in his name. But his word was in mine heart as a burning fire shut up in my bones, and I was weary with forbearing, and I could not stay" (Jer. 20:9). Jeremiah had in his soul a burning fire that did not go out.

I wish it were not so, but unfortunately most of us from time to time become discouraged in ministry. Just as a furnace has a small pilot light that ignites the furnace, so the "pilot light" never went out in Jeremiah's soul. When Jeremiah faced discouragement or disappointments, he did not quit on God. Similarly, we must do our best to keep the fire burning in our souls even at those times when we face discouragement and disappointments.

Every bus director and worker has times of disappointment. Perhaps a worker quit or failed to show up to carry out his responsibility. Perhaps we were even let down by someone in leadership. Maybe our "best kid" quit, or a teenager fell into sin. Maybe the parents of one of your children decided that they were not going to allow their child to ride the bus anymore. Although we all face times of discouragement, we cannot quit the important work God has called us to do. In fact, we must do all we can to guard against discouragement to ourselves as well as to those who follow us.

How does it happen? Why do we get overtaken at times by

discouragement? Let's examine some reasons that I have observed in workers in my experience in the ministry.

1. Focusing on problems rather than progress. Every bus ministry has problems, but we must deal with them rather than dwelling on them. Each week we have a staff meeting which is a time when we take care of problems. We present them, explain them, discuss them, and then offer possible solutions to them. We do not dwell on them, but we deal with them in a positive and proactive manner. Rather than dwelling on these problems throughout the week, we deal with them at this appointed time.

2. Talking about problems with others. This creates more problems than it ever fixes. Never speak about a problem with those who cannot solve it nor do anything about it. This often causes a problem to be exaggerated, blown out of proportion. Then the problem becomes gossip as it spreads to others who do not need to know about it. Bus worker, stay positive in your conversation to and from the routes and at bus meetings and in general talk with other workers. When problems are discussed in a "free for all" manner, they tend to bring blame and criticism that causes hurt feelings. Only tell those above you in a position of responsibility about the problem.

3. Poor communication. Workers need to attend bus meetings to learn the things that will often prevent problems. Bus directors must communicate every detail of special days, promotions, instructions, safety information, and other things that are expected of workers. The bus captain must then communicate these to his workers. Have plenty of reminders of times, schedules, promotions, work expected, and all that is involved. Poor communication is a huge cause of discouragement in the bus ministry.

4. No program or control on the bus ride. As much as the program on the bus is for the kids, it is also for the workers. A sure way to have discouragement among your workers is to have mayhem on the bus because no program was planned or because rules have not been enforced. No one likes to exclude riders from a bus route, but it is vital to have control on the bus ride. It is better to exclude rowdy riders than to discourage your workers and lose other well-behaved children.

5. Workers not feeling appreciated. Everyone needs to feel he is appreciated and needed. Recognition to a worker is a way of letting him know that he is needed. Do not take people for granted, or they may become discouraged. I know we are all supposed to serve the Lord with the right motives, but leaders need to recognize the importance of appreciating faithful workers. Do not leave the drivers out of this. Theirs can be a thankless task, but what would we do without them?

Pastors should recognize faithful bus workers. Each Sunday night I give a brief bus report to our people recognizing special milestones or achievements of workers or routes. Once a year we award a nice blue jacket to each bus captain who had one hundred riders on a Sunday during the previous year. We also award various plaques and trophies for the achievements of the workers, captains and drivers. I believe these seemingly small ideas can prevent a lot of discouragement.

6. Lack of a personal walk with God. In everything we do to encourage our workers, one thing on which we place an emphasis is having a strong personal walk with God. The bus ministry is a challenging ministry. It is certainly a spiritual work which means it requires a worker to have a daily personal walk with God. As leaders, we need to encourage our workers to have a time of personal Bible reading, prayer and fellowship with the Lord.

7. No new riders. New riders are a great source of encouragement. Do you remember when you first started your route, the excitement you felt with every new rider who got on the bus and with everyone who got saved and baptized? Every week you had new kids on the bus and were seeing parents trust Christ. After awhile you got so busy caring for the riders you had that you neglected getting new ones. That can be discouraging. Go out and get ten new riders in the next few weeks and see if that doesn't lift your spirits again. Make it your goal to have new riders each and every month.

8. Fatigue. We all get tired. Be careful that you understand the difference between fatigue and discouragement. Fatigue is when your body is tired or worn out, and it can lead to discouragement. Take care of yourself. Get enough rest. Eat right. Exercise. A healthy worker is usually a motivated worker.

Preventive medicine is always better than curative. You can either wait until you are discouraged, or you can do the right things to ward off discouragement. Either way, take heed to these things and avoid being a casualty of discouragement. Those kids and their families need you.

MAINTAINING A
GOOD SPIRIT

F EW THINGS will destroy a bus route, a bus ministry, a Sunday school class, or even a church as quickly as a bad attitude—or as we call it, a **bad spirit**. Our spirit affects people in ways we may not fully realize. It has been said that "Attitude is everything." I guarantee that it is of vital importance in ministry. Maintaining the right spirit is paramount to having success in your bus ministry and on your bus routes.

A preacher told me his personal story. He grew up in a very bad home environment. His father was so filled with hatred and bitterness that he seldom called his son by his name. Instead he used curse words when speaking to his young son. It was so bad that there were times he looked for pills in the medicine pantry to end his life. Instead, he would think about the bus people who visited him every Saturday and picked him up for church every Sunday morning. He thought of the kindness, love and the respect with which they treated him. To him it was a blessing just to hear someone call him by his name.

The bus workers knew nothing of the abuse, anger and hatred he endured because he never told them. He was embarrassed for them to know that his home was that bad or that his heart was broken to the point of considering suicide. Occasionally he took out his hurt by misbehaving on the bus. It was the spirit of those workers that kept him from hurting himself. It was their spirit that caused him to give his life to Christ and eventually led him into the ministry. I wonder if at times those workers were struggling with their own hurts and difficulties, but rather than allowing it to show, they kept a good spirit for that young man and the others who rode their bus. Little did they know the impact they were having on him.

The same is true on every bus that picks up children and teens across this nation. Little boys and girls, who are hurting for reasons about which you may never know, will ride your bus. The spirit on that bus may make all the difference in the world to them. Hearing their names spoken in a loving and caring manner may mean more than you can imagine. Having worked in the bus ministry for these many years, let me assure you that your good spirit is not negotiable. You must maintain it even when you may have hurts in your life. By the way, the Bible commands that we do.

> *"But now ye also **put off all these**; anger, wrath, malice, blasphemy, filthy communication out of your mouth.*
>
> *"Lie not one to another, seeing that ye have **put off the old man** with his deeds;*
>
> *"And have **put on the new man**, which is renewed in knowledge after the image of him that created him:*
>
> *"Where there is neither Greek nor Jew, circumcision nor uncircumcision, Barbarian, Scythian, bond nor free: but Christ is all, and in all.*
>
> *"Put on therefore, as the elect of God, holy and beloved, bowels of mercies, kindness, humbleness of mind, meekness, longsuffering;*
>
> *"Forbearing one another, and forgiving one another, if any man have a quarrel against any: even as Christ forgave you, so also do ye.*
>
> *"And **above all these things put on charity**, which is the bond of perfectness."*—Col. 3:8–14.

Every morning when we get up, we make a decision as to what clothing we are going to put on and wear that day. It is a choice we must make. The illustration is clear in this passage that just as we decide what we put on in the morning, we are to decide what spirit and behavior we put on for that day.

Have you ever looked in the mirror after you had gotten

dressed and realized what you were wearing was not appropriate for the day? What did you do? You "put off" the clothes you had first selected and then "put on" clothing you felt was more appropriate.

That is what we are to do as Christians. We are to "put off" certain attitudes and behaviors and "put on" ones more acceptable for a Christian. Bus workers must realize this every day but especially when going to work on the bus route. On any given Sunday, your demonstrating attitudes that are inappropriate for a Christian may have an eternally adverse effect on one who rides your bus.

Do you remember that preacher who told the story of his childhood? What if those faithful bus workers had forgotten to "put off" the wrong things and "put on" the right ones? Without knowing it, they were influencing eternity by their behavior and attitudes. We must take the time to put off things that will be detrimental, such as anger, wrath, malice, blasphemy, and filthy communication.

Then, we must put on that which is better, such as tender mercies, kindness, humbleness of mind, meekness, long-suffering, forbearance, forgiveness, and above all, charity.

One of my favorite preachers of the past was Vance Havner. Every year he preached in California when the roses were in full bloom. He loved roses, so early every morning he went out to the rose garden to pray and meditate. One morning a group of pastors were in the lobby of the motel ready to go to the services when Vance Havner walked in from the rose garden. One of them said, "Brother Havner, I know where you have been this morning. You have been in the rose garden. I can smell the sweet aroma of the roses." Likewise, our spirit should let people know that we have been with the Lord Jesus. Our bus riders should be able to experience the sweet spirit of the Lord Jesus when they ride the bus.

The effectiveness of your bus route will be determined by this in several ways.

1. Your spirit will determine the attitude and atmosphere of your bus route. Sometimes we wonder why our route does not have the same spirit as it did the previous week. Maybe it is because of what you "put on" that morning or even what you forgot to "put off." Show me a bus route whose workers have great spirits, and I will show you a bus route that has a great attitude on the bus. Don't be too quick to blame the riders. Maybe it would be different if your spirit were right.

2. Your spirit will determine the altitude of your bus route. There is a common denominator I have noticed in bigger bus routes. They have a great spirit on the bus brought about by the spirit of the workers. Groom your spirit and grow your route. Neglect your spirit, and your route will decline. Jesus always had a great spirit, and the result was that He attracted throngs of people. The same will be true of us if we work at having the Spirit of Christ.

3. Your spirit will determine the aptitude of your bus route. Are those who ride your bus growing in their love of the Lord and their knowledge of the Bible? It may be because of your spirit. In fact, it probably is. If your spirit is right, the people on your bus will grow in the Lord and learn better. One of the things teachers learn is how to create a good environment in their classroom. The atmosphere determines the capability of the students to learn. That is true on bus routes as well.

4. Your spirit will determine your amplitude on your bus route. When we want to be heard in a greater way, we may use an amplifier. Your spirit is an amplifier that speaks with greater volume to the hearts of those riders. Bus captains and workers with the best spirits have the best influence on their riders. If you truly want to influence others for Christ, be careful what you "put on." Amplify your message with your spirit.

Many years ago I decided to be around men who had what I wanted to have in my ministry. The first thing I noticed about these greatly used men of God was their spirit. I watched them and saw that they had "put off" things that other men had not. I also began to notice that they had "put on" things that others had not. They did not do it sometimes or occasionally. They did it consistently and on purpose. It was not because it was natural to them more than to others. It was because they had made a commitment to having the spirit that would allow God to use them in the greatest way possible.

Bus worker, if you want God to use you in a greater way to touch the potential future preachers, preachers' wives, Christian school teachers, and soul winners who are now embodied in those children and teens who ride your bus, look in the mirror and examine your spirit. Maybe there are some things you need to "put off" and others you need to "put on." Believe me, it makes all the difference in the world and, more importantly, for eternity.

III

THE PRINCIPLES OF THE BUS MINISTRY

THE BUS RIDE
TO CHURCH

IT IS Sunday morning and almost time to pick up the very first rider. For approximately the next hour you will be adding children to the bus until it is time to go to Sunday school. These kids will spend from an hour to as much as two hours riding the bus to and from Sunday school and church. They could have stayed at home and slept in or watched television. They did not have to come. There are two responsibilities every bus worker has during this time: (1) make the ride fun; (2) make the ride productive.

Every trip on the bus should be well planned in advance. The ride to and from church is a great opportunity to teach, preach, sing, make memories, and build closer relationships with the children. The bus captain should make certain there are no idle moments during the ride. You never know what program item it will be to which a child or teenager will respond. It may be that the ride to or from church will affect his life because of the singing, the testimonies, the lessons, or even just having fun with the workers. Plan and prepare for every opportunity in hopes that the children will respond for salvation, surrender or service.

A bus captain told me the story of a seventeen-year-old young man who rode his bus. He attended church and Sunday school, but it was on the bus ride home that the captain saw conviction in that young man's face. The bus driver pulled into an area to let some riders off, and the captain asked the young man if he would like to trust Christ as Saviour. He was ready to be saved. It was the ride home that "sealed the deal" and finished the work in the heart of that teenage boy. What if they had just let the kids sit there and no one had been leading in activities? Perhaps that young man would have stepped off that bus and never come to church again.

There are some important things for which to plan on your bus rides to and from church.

1. Prepare your spirit. The young people who ride your bus will detect and respond to your spirit. Make certain it is positive. Your attitude and spirit are vital in all you do for the Lord, but there will be weeks when you do not feel excited or positive. There will be weeks when you have problems or burdens. Do not allow your spirit to be affected. You can't fake it. You must maintain a good attitude.

◆ Have personal devotions to prepare your spirit.

◆ Keep your mind on the needs of the riders, not yourself.

◆ Ask the Lord for strength, wisdom and patience for the task at hand.

◆ Do not react to the behavior of the children. Lead them. Set a good example.

◆ Control your spirit. If you lose your temper with the children, you may lose them forever.

◆ Finish strong. Often bus workers have a great start but begin to get tired toward the end of the day. Don't allow Satan to ruin what the Lord has begun.

2. Prepare your bus in advance. Good leaders do not take anything for granted. They have an eye for detail. What if your wife prepared a meal but just as you all sat down to eat, she discovered there were no clean dishes? An effective bus route is effective because of leadership that makes certain everything is ready with the bus itself.

◆ Secure and prepare your bus on Saturday.

◆ Make sure that the bus is operational and make necessary repairs.

- Have a clean bus. A dirty bus creates a bad spirit.
- Decorate the bus for special events.
- Have a schedule for workers to clean the bus each week.
- Have rules posted along with their penalties.

3. **Prepare your program.** Decide exactly what activities you are going to have both to and from church. Don't "wing it"! Kids can tell the difference between well-planned and impromptu programs. Have an order of activities just like the pastor has an order of service for the church service. You know approximately how much time the ride will be. Make sure to fill it with your program so that the kids won't start their own.

- Have special promotions, but do not promote anything until you have it in hand!
- Give out prizes for behavior or for just riding the bus.
- Pass out any handouts that you may have prepared for the day.

4. **Prepare the songs to sing on the bus.** Singing is vital because music plays such a huge part in all of our lives but especially in the lives of children and teens. The world wants to capture the hearts of kids through music, and we must not let the world do that. Do not allow the kids to pick the songs unless you plan in advance to do so. It is often because of unpreparedness that we call for riders' choices of songs.

- Do not rely on your memory.
- Have a list of different types of bus songs. Have some that are fast, some slow, some with motions, and some Scripture songs.
- Select who is going to lead the songs and make certain he knows them.

5. **Prepare your games.** Kids love to play games, and this is a great way to keep them occupied and having fun. You cannot just preach at them or even tell stories. There must be time for play. Games need to be safe for travel, but there are many exciting and fun games that will make your ride home a highlight of the day. Game time will leave a lasting memory in the minds of the children so that they will want to ride the bus again the following week.

◆ Games are usually best for the ride home.

◆ Promote the games you are going to play on your way to church.

◆ Make sure all the kids can participate.

◆ Make the playing of the game more exciting than the winning of the game.

6. Prepare Bible verses to teach and memorize. Take advantage of the bus ride to teach verses that could help them in their daily lives. We must help them hide God's Word in their hearts. This can even be included as a game on the ride home.

7. Be faithful with your bus ride program. Do not get lazy and forget to make plans. Don't leave it to your workers to throw something together. You worked hard to get those children to ride your bus. Don't negate all that work with a sloppy program.

The last child has just stepped off the bus. It was a good day, and there were many blessings. You are tired but strengthened by your service to the Lord. Now is a good time to take inventory of your day. Ask yourself,

◆ Did the children have a fun and exciting time?

◆ Did they know that we love them and care about them?

◆ Did we teach them some new lessons from the Bible?

◆ Did they learn songs they will remember through the week?

◆ Did God work in their lives?

◆ Will they want to come back next Sunday?

If you could answer yes to all those questions, then you can know that it was a successful day and that you did your job faithfully.

THE POWER OF BEING PROACTIVE

FROM time to time I will hear from a pastor whose bus ministry has brought on a very critical problem that has caused great difficulties to the church. He will say something like, "Brother Fugate, I just felt we had to cut back on the bus ministry," or worse yet, "Brother Fugate, we had to make a tough decision and get out of the bus ministry for the time being." That is what happens when we are reactive rather than proactive. When I hear something like this, it makes me want to ask them if they cut back on their children or got rid of their families altogether when they had challenges or difficulties in their homes.

There will be challenges and difficulties in the bus ministry. I did not say that there **might** be. I said there **will** be challenges and difficulties. In fact, the bus ministry will bring on problems that are unique to that ministry.

Many pastors and bus directors make the mistake of being reactive when it comes to these problems. That is a huge mistake. You do not have to wait for a problem in order to be prepared for it. Being proactive is learning to act rather than to react; it is to take the lead in activity. Proactive bus ministries understand that to be successful you must attempt to anticipate potential problems before they ever arise. The goal is to be able to do one of three things: (1) prevent them; (2) minimize them; (3) or deal with them.

If we are proactive, some problems can be prevented; others can be minimized. Unfortunately, there are problems that we cannot prevent or minimize; but if we do not react, we can deal with them with the least possible amount of damage. Pastor, there will be challenges in the bus ministry.

◆ Financial (Gas and insurance aren't cheap.)

◆ Behavioral (Kids will be kids.)

◆ Accidental (wrecks)

◆ Mechanical (breakdowns, flat tires, etc.)

◆ Weather (Ice and snow happen, at least they do in Kentucky.)

◆ Logistical (Some bus routes are in a bit rougher neighborhoods.)

If you want to be successful in the bus ministry, you must be proactive in each of these areas and others as well. The first step in being proactive is ***preparedness.*** For example, we must have the buses prepared as much as possible. That means on Saturday they should be checked mechanically and filled with gas. The program for the bus rides needs to be well organized by having a list of songs, a list of Bible memory verses, props prepared, candy in hand, games chosen and prepared, workers informed and prepared, and such like. Being prepared is important and is the first step to being proactive.

Another aspect of being proactive is ***leadership.*** Being proactive means that we take the lead. Every effective bus ministry has leadership in more than one aspect of the ministry. In other words, a proactive bus ministry is built by people who know how to be in control of things and are willing to be responsible.

The pastor must lead. As pastor I work to keep things moving along in the church service, or in the order of service. I do not like a single moment of dead time. I have each service organized with an order of service that keeps things moving from the time the choir opens to the closing prayer.

However, I am also the leader of the bus ministry. I delegate, but that does not mean I am not the leader of the bus ministry and every other ministry in my church. I am the overseer of the church where God has made me pastor. Pastors who simply delegate and then become totally alienated from their ministries are failing to do their job.

The bus ministry must be led, first of all, by the pastor. Pastor, if your church survives the problems that arise from having a bus ministry, your church members must know that you are leading.

The bus director must lead. While the pastor is the overseer of the church, the bus director is the overseer of his ministry. He is not a soloist. He is part of the ensemble of leaders who assist the pastor in carrying out the ministries of the church. His job is to lead the bus ministry under the guidance of the pastor, but he **must** be a leader in his area of responsibility.

◆ Accept and accentuate what the pastor says. Carry out his vision. Be a team player.

◆ Anticipate problems the ministry faces and make certain you communicate them to the pastor with potential solutions and then to the workers with the solutions.

◆ Articulate his goals as those of the pastor.

◆ Assimilate the things needed to carry out the promotions on the buses.

◆ Accommodate the needs of your workers.

◆ Alleviate potential conflicts among workers.

◆ Administrate the details of all aspects of the bus ministry.

The bus captains must lead. If you are a bus captain, you are an overseer of a group of people whom God has entrusted to your care. Every Sunday you are taking the precious lives of children under your care. You cannot just show up and expect everything to go well. You must make certain that you lead your route. Bus captain, so many of the problems that could discourage you could be prevented if you were proactive; and part of that is, you must be the leader on your bus route. Your workers are looking to you. Your bus riders are looking to you.

One of the most important areas where a captain must be proactive is the activity time on the bus. We must get the riders busy doing what we want them to do rather than waiting for boredom to tempt them to misbehave. We cannot allow the children to be in charge and the workers to react. Many problems can be prevented if we are proactive in this area alone. Be the leader, bus captain, and make certain the program is well prepared and effective.

1. **Being proactive keeps everyone engaged in the proper program.**

2. **Being proactive is the most effective tool in preventing bad behavior,** or discipline problems.

3. **Being proactive is work.** However, I would rather work hard to keep control than to react in an attempt to fix problems.

4. **Being proactive keeps things moving.** This is far more exciting to the riders than just "winging it" and hoping things turn out well.

5. **Being proactive requires others to be involved.** Make certain that the workers on your bus are prepared and organized.

6. **Being proactive helps even during times of disturbance.** There will be disturbances, but these can handled better if everyone else is busy enjoying the program.

7. **Being proactive keeps the leaders excited and involved.** It will prevent them from behaving as mere baby-sitters.

Often laziness is really complacency. Complacency often comes when we are not thinking and planning ahead. That is when problems arise. With problems we often have reactions, which usually bring more problems. Proactive people are seldom complacent. They are sharper, more aware, more involved, more active, and more in control of situations. We can save ourselves a lot of heartache and difficulties by getting more proactive in our bus ministries. Be prepared. Be a leader. If you do, then you can better enjoy the blessings of your bus ministry.

WORKING WITH
BUS TEENS

W HEN A young person reaches his teenage years, it often becomes more difficult to maintain his interest in and eventually his faithfulness to church. Even ones who have ridden our buses for a long time often begin to feel that they have become "too cool" to ride the bus. Sometimes they even begin to create problems on the bus. To deal with this problem, we started a new ministry called the teen van route ministry. This ministry encourages teenagers to remain faithful to church and is designed to meet their needs.

We have a "B" Sunday school program, but when the bus kids become teenagers they become a part of the "A" Sunday school and attend our main church service. The teen van routes have been a great addition and blessing and have allowed us to be more effective in keeping teenagers faithful to church. After investing many years in their lives, we want to do whatever we can to keep these young people in church and growing in the Lord. There are certain things we do on the teen van routes that help us to be more effective. These things may help you as well.

1. Keep it exciting. One of the main reasons teenagers stop riding the bus is that they are not excited anymore. The promotions that once worked when they were five years old no longer work when they are fifteen. Make sure promotions and activities are geared for their age group. Teenagers still want to be a part of something that is fun and dynamic, but they have a different idea of what is exciting. Have workers who understand this fact and who are effective in making things exciting for teens.

2. Be persistent. You will need to hit the ground running with a teen van route. This is especially true if a young person has already missed church for a few weeks. You may repeatedly go by to pick him up only to be told that he is still sleeping and is not coming. Don't let that stop you. Keep going and keep building a relationship with that teenager. Eventually your persistence will pay off, and he will come because he knows you care about him. Teenagers can appear scary, but remember they are still kids at heart who want someone who cares enough not to give up on them.

3. Be patient. It was so easy to get "little Jimmy" to bring his Bible and to sing; but now that Jimmy is older, it is not so easy. It is easy to become a little impatient. We want older Jimmy to respond like little Jimmy did. Keep in mind that teenagers face a lot more negative peer pressure and satanic attacks than ever before. The Devil is after them in every imaginable way in today's culture, using clothes, music, hairstyles, and relationships in an attempt to corrupt them. Be patient and continue loving and leading them even as they are going through these temptations and influences. Many teenagers can be salvaged if Christian leaders will understand the changes they are going through as they become older. Lead them, but don't push them, or you may push them away.

4. Be consistent. Nothing will damage your influence with a teenager like inconsistency. Teens can sniff out a phony faster than anyone else. They pay careful attention when you use words like *promise* and *prize*. When you promise something and do not do it, you lose their respect. Be faithful. Keep your promises. Have promotions in hand so that you do not inadvertently forget to do what you promised. Never promise anything you cannot fulfill. Always keep your word. By the time a young person has become a teenager, he has heard promises and lies and has realized that many people are not good at fulfilling their promises. Teens are watching you to see if you are like everybody else. Teachers, leaders and in some cases even parents have bribed them with and promised them things without ever coming through. You must be different if you want to influence them for God.

5. Keep a bus route flavor. Teenagers would never admit it, but they still love the songs, the silly games, and the fun things that we do on our buses. What they don't like is being outnumbered by children. Remember, it is not a senior citizens' ministry. It is a teen van route. Have fun. Sing bus songs, play some games, and have fun while on your way to church. The teens will love it.

6. Challenge them to grow. One of the greatest blessings of teen van routes is that they allow our bus teens to be around the teenagers from our church families. This allows them to see how they should dress, walk, talk, behave around adults, sing, and live the Christian life. They are challenged to learn the Bible and to witness for Christ. This brings our bus teenagers to a totally different level. Suddenly, the guys are wearing suits, the young ladies are wearing dresses, they are quoting Scripture, and they are winning their family and friends to Christ. Being with the teens from our church families elevates them to a new level of awareness of what the Christian life is all about.

7. Let them help on the van route. Teenagers get excited about something when they are a part of that something. Allow faithful teens to help you with the route. Take them visiting with you. They know where other teenagers live and could easily lead you to some great prospects. They could also write down names, go to the doors, lead the songs, greet visitors, or even teach a lesson. The more they can do to help, the more they will enjoy being a part because it becomes **their** ministry.

8. Never give up on them. I have heard it said that getting one teenager to attend is as difficult as getting ten children. I'm not sure if that ratio is exactly accurate, but I do know that the teen van route ministry takes hard work. It takes visitation, love, patience, time, and lots of teaching. You will need to pray for them and visit them faithfully. You will have some who are faithful and others who seldom attend, but remember that these were your bus kids. Even if they have not attended in a while, **never** give up on them. You could be their only hope to keep them from destroying their lives.

It is a great blessing to see a young person grow up on the bus route, stay connected with the teen ministry, and then go to Bible college. We have had many young people who were reached through the bus ministry as children and whom we were able to keep faithful through the teen van routes. Knowing they are in the will of God and in Bible college preparing for ministry is a thrill because that is what the bus ministry is all about.

MISTAKES TO AVOID

LITTLE foxes spoil the vines, and nowhere is that more true than in our work with children. At times well-meaning workers do certain things that end up having terribly adverse effects on those who ride their buses. These could be avoided if they were made aware of them. While none of these are issues that will hurt immediately, they are things that will hurt us in the long run. Here are some I have seen.

1. Making promises that you cannot keep. Never promise anything you have not thought through, planned out and purchased ahead of time. Never promise something that you do not know you can provide. Sometimes in excitement or immaturity bus workers or captains will make promises that they are not able to keep. Make sure that every promise you make has been preapproved by the proper authority and is available or possible. Children often grow up in a world of broken promises. Church should be one place where promises are kept and trust is built, not broken.

◆ Do not promise things you cannot afford.

◆ Do not promise things the pastor would not or has not approved.

◆ Do not promise things that take time you do not have.

◆ Do not promise things that may not be available.

◆ Do not promise things you have not thought through thoroughly.

♦ Do not make impulsive promises.

♦ Do not overpromise and then underdeliver.

♦ Do not promise things you cannot fulfill quickly. "Hope deferred maketh the heart sick" (Prov. 13:12).

2. **Missing too many Sundays.** For bus captains and workers to be effective, faithfulness is vital. Faithfulness includes every part of your responsibility as a bus worker. Certainly workers need proper time for family vacations or sickness; but if you allow yourself to begin missing here and there, before long you will begin to affect the entire route and hurt the riders on your bus. Be faithful to bus meetings, to visitation, to ride the bus to and from church, to be a good example, and to invest time in the riders of your bus.

3. **Poorly trained workers.** Training sessions are imperative for each worker in his area of responsibility. Training is more than teaching. Teaching is done at a specific time in a setting where practical instruction is given. This is a must in every phase of the bus ministry. Innocent mistakes are often made by a worker who is trying to do right but has had little or no training. A leader has no right to be upset if proper training was not given. Who needs to be trained?

♦ Every bus captain needs to be trained.

♦ Everyone who visits on a bus route needs to be trained.

♦ Everyone who does personal work needs to be trained.

♦ Everyone who runs a bus program needs to be trained.

♦ Every driver needs to be trained.

4. **Temperamental behavior.** Leaders who are on an emotional roller coaster with their riders will destroy their routes as well as the people who ride them. Leadership is more than just teaching truths with our words. It is also teaching to have the right attitude. How can you do this if your attitude is up and down? I have seen workers destroy their routes because they could not control their own spirit. We cannot allow that in the leadership of the bus ministry. We cannot have a "can do" attitude one week and a "give up" attitude the next. It is important to keep an even spirit at all times.

◆ Stay positive and upbeat.

◆ Stay joyful.

◆ Stay encouraging.

◆ Stay levelheaded.

◆ Stay believing.

5. Changing schedules. There are times in every area of our lives when schedules must be adjusted. However, if you are constantly changing the times for bus meetings, the times for bus visitation, the times the bus runs on the route, and the times you return home with the riders, you are sending a message that other things are more important than the bus ministry. Things that are important operate on a firm schedule. Make certain to choose times that are convenient, practical and effective for everyone involved, and then stay with them. This provides stability for the workers, the bus riders and for everyone involved.

◆ Set your schedule.

◆ Make sure everyone knows the schedule.

◆ Stay on schedule.

6. No program on the bus. You could add here a poorly planned program because that also will hurt your bus route. The ride is at least half of the excitement of a bus route. This is a time for the kids to begin to learn and to enjoy the ride to and from church. Bus routes that have no singing, games, fun, teaching, and instruction on the ride to and from church will not be as productive as those that do. The bus program can and should be the most exciting part of the day for the bus riders.

◆ Learn to run a good program.

◆ Keep that program exciting and fun!

◆ Involve everyone in the program from the workers to the riders—drivers excluded. (It's their job to drive the buses.)

The years of working with bus workers has taught me something very important. When we mess up in the little things, we experience less success. When we experience less success, we become discouraged. When we become discouraged, we lose our heart for the route. When we lose our heart, we quit. Do not risk your work for God by being careless. Take heed of these little areas, and the results will be evident.

REACHING THE PARENTS
OF YOUR BUS RIDERS

PRAISE the Lord for the many children reached through bus ministries across America. The future lives and eternal destiny of many have been changed because of faithful bus workers' reaching these children and teenagers. However, another great aspect of an effective bus ministry is reaching the parents of these children. We must not forget to emphasize the importance of reaching out to these moms and dads. You could give no greater gift to a bus child than a Christian home.

Reaching parents is far more difficult and time-consuming than reaching children. The greatest harvest is children. D. L. Moody began his ministry by reaching the toughest children in Chicago. The majority of people we reach will be won to Christ when they are young. However, we cannot simply overlook the importance of reaching out to the parents of our bus children. God has blessed our church with many adults coming to the Lord as a result of our efforts. Many have grown in the Lord and now provide a Christian home to their families. Here are some things we have found to be effective in reaching parents.

1. **Compassion for them.** Compassion means to share the hurt or pain of another. It causes us to enter emotionally into the needs of another. If we want to reach these parents, we must have a sincere compassion for them to trust Christ as their Saviour; to show them, teach them and encourage them in the importance of following the Lord in believer's baptism; and to spend time

with them in their homes during the week teaching them how to have personal devotions and to grow in the Lord.

We give the adults a calendar with a daily Bible-reading schedule. We keep a list of all faithful class members, visitors and new contacts; and we pray for these people daily. I have found that the more you pray for someone, the more compassion you will have for him.

2. Communicate with them. It is not enough merely to see the multitudes; we must reach out to them and communicate with them. Every person who attends Sunday school or church fills out an information card that includes giving us his name, address, email address, phone number, children's names, birthdays, and anniversary. This allows us to send emails to keep him informed as to what is going on in Sunday school and keep him informed of church events and activities.

- Spend time with the parents.
- Let them get to know who you are.
- Tell them what goes on at church.
- Talk to them about their children.
- Let them know that you are there for them.
- Call and check on them.
- Send text messages to let them know you are thinking about and praying for them.
- Learn their names and their children's names.
- Send cards to them on special occasions in their lives.

Great builders are effective communicators. Become effective at doing this with the parents, and you will build familiarity and trust with them. If they trust you, they will be more likely to listen to you or to turn to you when difficulties arise in their lives.

3. Connect with them. The Gospel of John, chapter 5, tells us of an impotent man who lay next to the pool at Bethesda with a disease that had plagued him for thirty-eight years. Jesus asked him if he would like to be made whole, but He did not stop there. Jesus listened to the man's excuses; and when he was finished, He gave the man direction. Likewise, we are letting people know we care by getting to know more about them, calling them, and sending notes to let them know we are thinking about them and praying for them. In doing so we are making a connection. People are selfish but not always in a bad way. They merely want someone who takes an interest in their interests.

◆ Listen to what they enjoy, gratifying their desire to talk about themselves.

◆ Visit them weekly when they first attend.

◆ Introduce them to the teacher when they come to Sunday school.

◆ Tell people something about them that is not personal, like where they work. They will be impressed that you remember.

◆ Introduce them to other faithful couples in the class. We have a light breakfast before class begins where we serve coffee, milk and juice. This provides an opportunity to introduce them to others. Watch their interaction with others to see with whom they seem best to connect.

◆ Encourage other adults to make a personal visit to them. This helps the bus parents to become familiar with other people and better connects them to your church.

◆ Help them feel a connection with the pastor. Tell them a few things about the pastor so that they feel a connection to him. Humanize him by letting them know he is a real and genuine person. Then take time to introduce them to him personally. Let the pastor know who they are. I know most of our faithful bus children; therefore, when a parent is introduced to me, it gives me a chance to say something positive about his child or children. That makes a great connection with parents. If the pastor cares enough to know who their child is, that makes a huge impression on them.

Someone once said that people will not connect to you until you first connect with them. Make the effort to connect to the parents of the children who ride your buses, and many of them will not only trust Christ but will begin serving the Lord as well.

4. **Confidence in your purpose.** We must believe in people

and in the power of God working in their lives.

◆ Let people know you believe in them and that they are a blessing to you. A parent who allows his children to ride your bus to church should know you are thankful and that you respect him for doing so.

◆ Parents of bus children should never be made to feel inferior because they do not take their kids to church or because their circumstances are not lofty.

◆ Learn how to make people feel special. Find things for which you can compliment them. All of us need others to encourage and believe in us. As God's people, we must be builders of people.

There are very few things as exciting as watching the face of a child when his parents come to church for the first time and he gets to introduce them to his leaders. Some of these kids have never known what it was like to go to church with their moms or dads. Even more exciting is to see their faces when their moms or dads walk down the aisle professing their faith in Christ and being baptized. The bus ministry helps to make this happen if we remember that everybody has a hungry heart and that we are to reach everybody with the Gospel. When people know you love them and care for them, they will respond. Love is the greatest gift and motivator to the heart of anyone. To reach out to one with a hurting heart and to help him grow in Christ is the greatest joy and reward of all.

SAFETY ON THE BUS

PARENTS want to know "Is my kid safe on the bus?" Never forget that. When you get a parent's permission for his child to ride your bus, he is entrusting his child's well-being into your care. Your opportunity to influence these kids eternally is at stake. If you do not provide a safe environment on your bus, you are placing your entire ministry in jeopardy. In fact, you may be placing the entire bus ministry at risk if you are not safety minded.

We are commanded to reach as many people as we can, but we must reach them safely. We should operate our bus route with the same safety and organization we would want for our own children. When I send one of my children on a church activity, I want to know who is in charge, who is driving, and that the activity is going to be safe.

The two key elements of safety are being properly prepared and proactive. If you wait for things to happen, they will. If you prepare and take action ahead of time, you can prevent many potential safety issues. Awareness is a major element in safety. Here are a few safety guidelines that should be helpful.

1. Prepare your bus. There are a few simple things that you can do to provide safety for the children. Most church buses are used, so it is important to perform regular maintenance on the buses in order to keep them up to code, making them safe for the children. Do not neglect the upkeep of your buses.

Make sure the buses are clean inside and that everything is

in order. A dirty bus promotes disarray and misbehavior, while a clean bus promotes organization and safety. Decorating your bus can also cause the children to want to obey the rules and stay in their seats.

Make certain that the emergency exits are working properly. You hope never to need them, but they should be up to code with your city and/or county. Look for and take care of any sharp edges on your bus by making certain your seats have seat covers on them or by covering them with duct tape. A child could easily fall and be cut or seriously injured by bare steel that is pointed or sharp. Eventually someone is going to fall while on a bus, so make certain that the seat does not make his fall worse by causing a serious wound. You can purchase colored duct tape that looks nice and pad the sharp edges with it. This is not just common sense. It is the law! The bus should be in the same condition that you would expect for your children.

> **Note:** *Church Bus News* sells a "Driver's Daily Log" that you can purchase to assist you in keeping your bus up to code. The log has a checklist in it of things that **must be checked regularly according to federal law**.

2. Prepare your workers and drivers. Safety is every worker's business. Every worker needs to be aware of the children's safety and prepared to take action in order to keep the children safe.

It is also required by federal law that every driver have a CDL license with a passenger endorsement. By the way, listen to your driver. His word must be final when it comes to safety on the bus. The driver's main purpose is to transport riders to and from church safely. His one and only purpose is to drive that bus. Do not allow him to be distracted.

Have regular safety meetings with your workers to remind them of the procedures that involve safety. Do not assume they will remember everything. Refresh their memories on a regular basis.

Another idea is to make certain there is someone who knows and can administer CPR in the case of an emergency. You never know when this might be needed.

3. Prepare a safety system. Imagine the terror of discovering you have lost a child. Every child should get his hand marked as he gets on the bus. This helps to make certain everyone gets back on the same bus which he rode to church. Have the name, address, names of parents, and contact number for every child on your bus. A backup number might even be a good idea. You must get into this practice. This is a potential legal issue for which you want to be prepared.

4. Prepare the kids. It is a good idea to give the children some instructions as to what to do in case of an emergency; however, the best way to practice good safety is always to be in control of the riders on your bus. You must be proactive in trying to fix problems before they happen. Such things as letting kids off the bus safely are vital. Do not allow them just to jump off the bus or cross the street on their own. Make certain you **know** they are safely inside their homes before you leave. Two things with which we deal in separate chapters but which are important to bus safety are

- the program on the bus;
- behavior and discipline.

Someone once said, "When dealing with people and problems, always act; never react." If you react to a problem, you might react wrongly and do or say something you shouldn't. Plan your responses so that when you respond, you are carrying out a prepared plan of action.

Safety could make or break your bus route and even your entire bus ministry. Do not make it an afterthought. Have safety procedures spelled out in advance and then drill your workers on their importance. Never allow anyone to ignore these important procedures.

TEACHING CHILDREN THE WORD OF GOD

WHILE the bus ministry is a wonderful tool for reaching children with the Gospel, it should also place a big emphasis on the teaching of the Word of God. Never assume that children cannot learn the Bible or that they don't have the desire to do so. Childhood is the best time of life to learn the Bible.

What a miracle and blessing that God has preserved His inspired words in the Bible! We should teach our children that the Bible is the perfect Word of God and encourage them to love and use the King James Bible.

If we are not careful, we will use all our time on the bus ride and in Sunday school having fun and playing games, leaving out the most important aspect which is teaching the Word of God to our children. Let me encourage you to make certain that with the games, the fun and the singing, you teach the Bible at all times. It is the Bible that gives a child guidance in life and for eternal life in Christ. "Thy word is a lamp unto my feet, and a light unto my path" (Ps. 119:105).

Paul reminded Timothy that he had known the Holy Scriptures since he was a child and they made him wise unto salvation. The Bible gave Timothy the understanding of being a sinner and needing a Saviour.

"But continue thou in the things which thou hast learned and hast been assured of, knowing of whom thou hast learned them;

*"And that from a child thou hast known the holy scriptures,
which are able to make thee wise unto salvation through faith
which is in Christ Jesus."*—II Tim. 3:14, 15.

I could give many Scriptures that show the importance of the
Bible in young people's lives, but my goal is to share ideas of **how**
to teach children the Word of God. There are several very effective
tools I recommend for all bus workers and teachers to master.

1. Visual aids. Your voice is not enough to imprint truth into
the minds of the riders on your bus. They need visuals to help
keep their attention and to reinforce what you are teaching. Simple poster boards with Scripture verses written on them are one
good way to teach children the Bible. You can also purchase or
make nice posters with verses printed on them and use them in
decorating the bus.

Let me encourage you to use printed Scripture for children to
see when you are teaching the Bible or memorizing Scripture.
You also will do well if you add graphics, like pictures of animals
or even characters, to your poster boards. Colors are also important. Remember these kids are accustomed to having bright and
exciting things put in front of them constantly on television. We
cannot expect them to respond to black-and-white or boring
visual aids.

2. Memorization. I have often wondered at how many times
an adult reaches a point in life where he has no place to turn and
suddenly remembers a Scripture he memorized as a child on a
bus route or in a Sunday school class. If he is saved, the Holy
Spirit is still in him and may bring that Scripture to mind just to
get him to return to the Lord. We have a great opportunity on
the bus route to instill Scriptures into the minds and hearts of
children.

Pick the verses ahead of time each week. Give prizes to those
who remember the memory verse for the week. This is a good
way to teach the purpose and reasons for the bus ministry to our
riders. Be sure to memorize verses that deal with certain matters
that are especially important in their lives.

- Verses on salvation
- Verses that teach everyone is a sinner

◆ Verses dealing with the penalty for sin

◆ Verses about the birth, sinless life, death and resurrection of Jesus

◆ Verses that instruct on how to receive Christ by faith into our hearts

◆ Verses about the goodness of God

◆ Verses about Christian principles

◆ Verses on important Bible doctrines

◆ Verses about overcoming temptation

◆ Verses about the dangers of sin

◆ Special verses on themes such as Christmas, Thanksgiving, Easter, etc.

◆ Verses that accompany a theme you are using in your promotion

3. Scripture songs. This is one of the most effective ways to teach Bible verses to children. It allows you to use two important tools—singing and repetition. It is amazing how easily children can memorize Bible songs, even at a very early age.

My wife and I have five children. It always amazes us how easily they learn songs. They learn Bible verses in song for which they do not yet understand the meaning. As they get older, they begin asking what the words mean. I love this method of teaching the Bible to children. It is amazingly effective.

4. Bible stories. Good storytellers are good communicators. If you want to keep the attention of those on your bus, learn not only how to tell a story but how to make it come alive. Act it out. Use your voice to change the pace, the volume and the tone of a story. Make the Bible come alive with good storytelling. Stories are a great way to teach truth. Even our Lord used stories to teach His disciples.

5. Bible games. There are many different games you can use. One simple yet great game is to cover the words on a poster board as the children memorize the verses. Read the verse from the poster board and then gradually cover up the words as you read through it several more times. This is an exciting way to learn.

Good games keep the fun on the bus ride but also allow you to teach God's Word.

6. Repetition. This is of critical importance. Repetition is the key to learning. The world uses this tool effectively, and so must we. Hearing the same Bible verses or truths over and over again can help us better to commit them to our long-term memory. Use different methods to teach the same truths and the same Scriptures. The more they hear the truth, the greater the chance it will have a permanent effect on their lives.

Bus worker, make certain that your mind-set is to get as much Bible inside the minds of these children as is possible in the time you have with them. Be creative and consistent in your emphasis of the Bible. Having fun is important in keeping the children coming back, but the real goal is teaching them the Bible. One day they won't be on the bus any longer. How much of God's Word will be hidden in their hearts because of your efforts? Never lose sight that their lives will be changed only if we use the fun and games to permeate their hearts and minds with the Scriptures.

FINANCES AND THE
BUS MINISTRY

OPERATING a church bus ministry certainly has expenses. However, if you are waiting for me to say that it is costly, you will be waiting a long time. I do not believe that a bus ministry is expensive compared to its productivity any more than FedEx® would consider a truck expensive in comparison to delivering packages by bicycles. Sure, bicycles are cheaper than trucks; but in the capacity of trucks to deliver more packages, there is no comparison. The same is true with a bus ministry. It is not expensive when taken in the context of its potential productivity.

Some pastors want to have a bus ministry, but their commitment is not strong enough to take on the added expenses. They have not yet just decided to do it. The challenge for many is in making the initial decision to get started. Let me illustrate this.

Some parents see the benefit of sending their children to a Christian school but consider its cost and decide that it is a luxury they cannot afford. Other parents see the exact same benefits but see it as a necessity they cannot neglect, no matter what the cost. Both understand the need of getting their children under the influence of Christian teaching, but the difference is in their commitment to pay the price.

The same is true with many pastors when it comes to the bus ministry. One sees the cost as a determining factor as to whether or not he will run buses. Another sees the cost as the price he is willing to pay to accomplish the task of getting out the Gospel. A pastor who commits to the bus ministry finds a way to pay the cost. The other does not. It is a matter of making the choice. Once a church makes the choice to have a bus ministry, they will find a way to finance it.

1. **There are two parts of a church:**

- The church, which is the people;
- The ministries, which are the work the people do to serve the Lord.

Everyone in the church makes up the first one. Each ministry, however, starts and operates from that first one, the church. That is why we call them ministries of the church. The church comes first. The ministries follow. Pastors sometimes make the mistake of placing the ministries of the church above the church itself. The result is often an unhealthy church and even people that feel neglected and thus become disgruntled. I am the pastor of the church. I am the leader of the ministries. Both are important parts of my duties.

2. **The church provides the finances and the facilities for the ministries.** A healthy church can support ministries better than ministries can support a church. In fact, ministries that feel they no longer need the church often become trouble to the pastor. These ministries begin to believe that they are more important than the church as a whole. Parachurch ministries can especially be guilty of this. It is good for the ministries to stay in need of the church. The minute they no longer need the church, rebellion can begin to develop.

3. **The goal is for the ministries to increase.** Growing churches need more places for ministry, and good ministries help churches to grow. Pastor, be careful that you do not start ministries before the church is ready. There is a balance to growth that must be maintained. With that having been said, it should be our desire to begin new ministries as the need arises.

4. **In order for the ministries to increase, the church must increase.** This is so important. A ministry reaches out beyond the church but inevitably should help build the church. However, a

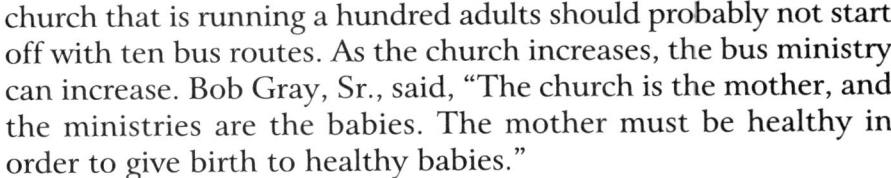

church that is running a hundred adults should probably not start off with ten bus routes. As the church increases, the bus ministry can increase. Bob Gray, Sr., said, "The church is the mother, and the ministries are the babies. The mother must be healthy in order to give birth to healthy babies."

5. As pastor, my job is to see to it that both grow. The best way to grow is through soul winning. Some pastors want to build their churches through transfers; but when you do so, you are inheriting the problems of your members' past churches rather than getting to train your members yourself. I have never seen a healthy New Testament church that was built on transfers and then somehow magically became a soul-winning church. Soul winning is God's way to build a church. A church is the place of ministry. Ministry brings growth to the church which allows the church to further its ministry.

6. A healthy church cannot be determined by attendance or offerings alone. Those things may help gauge the health of a church, but they are not the truest way of knowing if a church is healthy. There are pastors who love to speak of their crowds and the size of their offerings. Those same pastors often have few ministries in which people are serving. The first part of the church is strong, but the ministry side is not. The purpose of the church is not attendance. It is equipping people for service.

7. The progression of the people's growth is important. Here is the progression.

- ◆ salvation
- ◆ baptism
- ◆ church membership
- ◆ ministry

Some pastors feel that the last step is Bible knowledge. However, what does the Bible say?

> *"For when for the time ye ought to be teachers, ye have need that one teach you again which be the first principles of the oracles of God; and are become such as have need of milk, and not of strong meat.*

"For every one that useth milk is unskilful in the word of right-eousness: for he is a babe."—Heb. 5:12, 13.

We are taught that maturity comes only to those who are involved in ministry. As the church grows, I want to take the growing Christians to maturity. To do so, I must lead them into ministry. My goal is to lead them as far as they are willing to go.

"And he gave some, apostles; and some, prophets; and some, evangelists; and some, pastors and teachers;

"For the perfecting of the saints, for the work of the ministry, for the edifying of the body of Christ."—Eph. 4:11, 12.

Church growth is both a means to an end and a by-product. We win souls and the church grows. We perfect the saints for the work of the ministry. The work of the ministry leads to church growth. Growth is not the end, but growth will come if we do the other properly.

8. As the church grows, the diversity of the ministries will also grow. Some young pastors go to a new area and immediately try to reach the poorest ghettos they can find. Men like Dr. Hyles effectively reached deeper into the ghetto more than most, but he did not start there. It was as the church grew that the diversity was able to grow as well. A soul-winning church should eventually be reaching every demographic group in their area. It may take time, but we must make certain to keep the church healthy in order to do so.

Operating bus routes has been a great way for Clays Mill Road Baptist Church to grow as a church and to expand our ministries. We have seen some exciting things happen as a result of maintaining a healthy balance in both parts of the church.

HOW TO FINANCE THE
BUS MINISTRY

THE BUS ministry is totally concerned with winning souls, baptizing our converts, and making disciples of the Lord Jesus Christ. As in any other endeavor to reach the lost with the Gospel, there are costs involved. Jesus and His disciples discussed the costs and expenses of the work of spreading the Gospel. I want to share some ideas and principles for financing the bus ministry. These ideas are what we have successfully implemented at Clays Mill Road Baptist Church.

1. **Designate money in the overall church budget for the bus ministry.** This budget item should be to cover the operating costs. Items such as the fuel, insurance and maintenance of the buses need to be included in this budget. It is our goal to add a five-percent cushion to our budget items, especially when the price of fuel fluctuates as it does.

◆ Fuel: The weekly cost for fuel for each bus can be calculated by multiplying the average number of miles your buses travel each week by the price of gas per gallon, then dividing that product by the miles per gallon that your average bus gets.

◆ Insurance: This price will vary based on a variety of factors. Consult your insurance agent for pricing.

◆ Maintenance: Maintenance cost will vary from week to week and is a factor that should not be overlooked.

2. **Budget for promotions.** We have a budget item designated

"Promotions." We not only budget for bus promotions but also all Sunday school promotions. This includes promotions for those who drive to church as well as those who ride buses. We figure an average of seventy-five cents per promotion per child for a bus promotion. Then we look at the planned promotions for the year and figure the cost of those as well.

Normally we conduct twenty sponsored Sunday school and bus promotions a year. This includes our six-week spring and fall attendance campaigns. That means we have twelve weeks of attendance campaigns with an additional eight planned promotions. There are some weeks we have a promotion that has no cost, such as Crazy Hat or Crazy Shoe Sunday, which I will explain in another chapter. Not all promotions have to be costly, but there will be costs involved in many, so we must plan ahead and budget for these.

3. Ask your people to designate money weekly or monthly to the bus ministry. Present the bus ministry in your church like a mission work. We do not use money from our missions giving to finance our bus ministry, but I do present a specific bus route as a missionary ministry to a neighborhood in our city. I believe that it is a missionary work, so I encourage our members to give designated money specifically to the bus ministry when possible.

4. Give good reports of the bus ministry to your members. Almost every Sunday evening I make some mention of the bus ministry and its results. I talk about people getting saved and about lives that have been changed because of the bus ministry. People will give when they know that their money is being used to reach people for Christ. That is what drives successful missions giving. When a missionary tells of the souls being won on a foreign field, people give more. The same thing happens when you report on your local field. Even during the summer months when attendance is at its lowest, lives are being transformed, and eternal destinies are being changed.

A word of warning: Be careful not to present to the church the problems or negatives of the bus ministry as if it were a nuisance. There is no work, no business, no industry or company that does not face difficulties at times. If it is worth facing problems to make money, it is certainly worth the difficulties to see souls saved and lives changed. If the people perceive it as a greater problem than blessing, they will be less inclined to support it.

5. Raise money for special days. For over twenty years we have conducted Christmas Party Sunday. On a Sunday morning I present the need for people to sponsor at least five to ten bus riders. This enables us to purchase a nice meal, a new Bible and a Christmas present for each bus rider. It costs about five or six dollars per child. In less than five minutes our members give several thousand dollars to finance this special day. It is always a highlight of our church year and draws a large crowd with multitudes of souls saved, including many parents of our bus children. This gives our members a way to help others during the Christmas season.

6. Take special offerings to purchase a new bus. A new bus is an item for which no money is designated in our budget. The Bible tells us that our hearts follow our money. Here is a way to accomplish two things at once.

- Raise additional money for a new bus.
- Get the hearts of your people behind the new route and the bus ministry in general.

Present the need for the new bus and the opportunity it will afford to win more souls to Christ, and then ask your people to give to help purchase the bus. Let them know exactly what amount is needed to do so.

7. Keep your church strong to finance ministries. It is imperative that we build a strong drive-in Sunday school so that we can finance ministries such as the bus ministry. The key is personal soul winning and winning adults to Christ. I am not referring to "marketing" to reach people but to personal, confrontational, door-to-door, person-to-person soul winning. God blesses the work of soul winning.

8. Let your community know about the bus ministry. I regularly communicate with our city's mayor, police chief, and other leaders regarding our bus ministry to keep them informed. I let them know of our purpose, our schedules, and the areas and streets where we are ministering. I also let them know of lives that are being changed because of our work in those neighbor-hoods. I tell them of our commitment to keep the children safe. We stress the importance of maintaining an open communication with the police, the parents and the people of our city. Businesses often make donations to help in the "community work" of our bus ministry.

These are basic ways to keep the bus ministry from draining your finances or from your church's being forced to cut back. It always grieves my heart when I hear of churches dropping bus routes for any reason but especially for financial reasons. If God led you to start a route, make certain that you have made finan-cial plans to keep it running. Cutting back would be like a cou-ple's having four children and then deciding they could afford only three or even two of them. They would find a way to make certain they did not orphan any of their kids. It is just as impor-tant that we do not orphan our bus route kids but rather dili-gently work at having the funds to finish the good work which we have begun.

DISCIPLINE ON
THE BUS

IT WON'T take long for those who work in the bus ministry to discover that it comes with its own challenges. Kids will not always be angels on the bus. In fact, they will often behave just the opposite. The questions asked most about the bus ministry are about discipline. This is a very important area of concern and one we should not take lightly. There must be a plan of action to care for discipline problems, or our emotions can lead to problems bigger than the bad behavior of a child. Preventing problems is much better than merely solving problems. When a child causes problems on the bus, everyone is affected, including the child, the workers and the other children on the bus.

1. Post a set of rules on the bus. The rules need to be posted where everyone can clearly see and read them. The rules need to be concise and complete. The rules will only serve as a foundation for a good bus ride, but they will not guarantee it.

The rules of a game allow us to play the game. The rules are not the purpose. For example, basketball is fun, but it has boundaries. The emphasis is not on those boundaries, but you cannot play the game without them.

The rules on the bus allow for the program to be conducted. The program is the purpose. The rules merely allow the program to fulfill its purpose of teaching, training and providing an enjoyable ride to church. You can find examples posted online of rules for most school districts in America. These will give you an idea of some good rules. The experience of running a church bus program will provide other rules that need to be posted and followed. I do not suggest having too many rules, but here is a list of things you may want to include.

- No hitting
- No cursing
- No running on the bus
- Everyone in a seat while the bus is in motion
- No arms and heads outside the windows
- No fighting
- No throwing of objects

2. **Rules should be read aloud each week by the captain and riders.** When everyone is on the bus, it is wise to read through the rules with the bus riders. It will serve as a good reminder and instill discipline in them. Make it fun. Let them read the rules out loud with you. Discipline provides security. Occasionally you should include the rules on your bus flier so that the parents know what rules and discipline are being enforced while their children are riding on the bus to and from church. Most parents appreciate proper discipline on the bus.

3. **Rules must be enforced, or they will become a problem rather than a solution.** If you do not enforce certain rules, then your riders will realize you are not serious about them. Many problems can be avoided if we deal with situations immediately rather than allowing them to grow.

4. **Let the riders know of the punishment for not keeping the rules.** Letting them know the punishment will cause them to be more reluctant to disobey the rules. Here are a few ideas for discipline.

- The first offence should be a loving word reminding them of the rule.
- If a child is out of control or will not follow the rules, it is best for the captain to go talk to the parents. Try to go that day if possible and let them know of the specific rule(s) that

were broken. This often corrects the problem quickly. Most parents want to be told if their children are not behaving. Most kids fear that as well.

> **Note:** Please remember the poor home lives in which many of our bus riders live. Many come from rough situations, and often a problem at home can cause them to misbehave on the bus.

◆ Take away a privilege. Whenever possible, it is best to give promotions at the end of the bus ride. Remind them of the promotion when they first get on the bus. Remind the riders that they can lose their promotion if they do not behave.

> **Note:** If this happens, be sure to let the parents know the true story so that the children do not make up a story about why they did not receive the promised promotion. You do not want the parents to distrust you.

◆ If problems persist, let them know they cannot ride the bus for two weeks. Meet with the parents to let them know about the offense and the decision you had to make. During those two weeks, be sure to visit them to assure them of your love. Often this causes children to become closer to the captain and provides a unique opportunity for a greater influence in their lives. When they learn of a promotion or a special day they are missing, it will also encourage good behavior when they return.

> **Note:** I do not recommend that you tell a rider that he can never ride the bus again. This could hurt him for the rest of his life. You may have to extend his suspension to a month or more, but never make it permanent. Always leave the door open for a return.

◆ Do not physically restrain a child, unless he is about to cause bodily harm to a worker or another child. Physical contact should be reported to the parents as soon as you get to the child's home.

◆ No child should be removed from the bus ministry without approval from the bus director.

◆ Learn how to instruct without threatening. Threats make bad situations worse.

◆ Don't yell or scream at a child. Bus children hear screaming at home or school, and they will not respond to it. Speak in a low, calm and slow manner.

◆ Pray for wisdom for each discipline problem.

◆ Pray with the child when you are forced to apply discipline.

5. Do not hold past bad behavior over their heads. Don't keep bringing it up. They may get that at home. Let them know that the past is the past.

6. Do not forget the value of positive discipline. We punish to correct, but we praise and reward to encourage. Sometimes just a word of praise will make a child want to be good. When a child who has been disciplined for doing wrong is subsequently praised for doing right, it can change his attitude entirely. Kids want to please. They especially want to please their leaders. Make sure you notice when they are good and they know it.

We were all kids once, and we were not angels all the time. Admit it. Do not forget what it is like to be a kid with all his energy and curiosity. Don't be an Old Fogey and make keeping the rules drudgery. Have them. Post them. Recite them. Enforce them. However, remember that the greatest means to a disciplined life is a changed life. If we can keep our bus kids coming, they will grow into well-behaved young people whose lives count for God.

FAITH PLEASES GOD

"But without faith it is impossible to please him: for he that cometh to God must believe that he is, and that he is a rewarder of them that diligently seek him."—Heb. 11:6.

THE essence of this chapter will determine the blessings in your work for God. Read the following seven statements. They may surprise you at first, but they are true.

◆ Working on a bus route does not necessarily please God.

◆ Driving a church bus and picking up little boys and girls for church does not necessarily please God.

◆ Being a bus captain does not necessarily please God.

◆ Going soul winning does not necessarily please God.

◆ Being the pastor of a church does not necessarily please God.

◆ Serving God in any capacity does not necessarily please Him.

Now before you quit doing the things listed above, please read the next seven statements, and I think you will better understand the purpose for this chapter.

◆ Working on a bus route by faith does please God.

◆ Driving a church bus and picking up little boys and girls for church by faith does please God.

- ◆ Being a bus captain by faith does please God.
- ◆ Going soul winning by faith does please God.
- ◆ Being the pastor of a church by faith does please God.
- ◆ Serving God by faith in any capacity does please Him.

The Bible makes these three things very clear.

1. The only way we can please God is by faith.

2. Without faith we cannot please God.

3. Anything we do that is not of faith is sin.

"And he that doubteth is damned if he eat, because he eateth not of faith: for whatsoever is not of faith is sin."—Rom. 14:23.

There is a danger for those who work in the bus ministry to become mechanical or methodical while forgetting that our work is not merely practical work. It is, in fact, a spiritual work. Many newer Christians start out doing something for God because they just want to serve. I think God counts that as faith. Their innocent desire to serve the Lord in some way is a show of their faith.

However, after serving in the bus ministry for a few years, we could start going through the motions, because we know what to do and how to do it, without having to give it much thought. We must never forget that it is God's work and every work for Him must be a work of faith. If it is not a work of faith, then it is sin. I would be remiss to write a book on the bus ministry and leave out this essential truth.

It is important to be organized and prepared, to visit our regular riders, to sign up new riders, to prepare the program on the bus, and to do all the other duties we have to do. However, we must not forget, ignore or overlook the importance of depending on God in our work. We want the children to enjoy the program and classes. However, the very purpose of our work is spiritual. We want every child we reach to be saved. We want the seeds of Bible truths to be planted in their hearts and minds so that they will grow in the Lord. Therefore, our work is more than practical or physical, and only by the Holy Spirit can such work be accomplished.

One of our workers told me about a nine-year-old girl who

rode the bus to Sunday school. She came from a very rough home life and lived in the midst of every imaginable sin and wickedness. She sat through Sunday school and children's church without trusting Christ as her Saviour.

A worker sat with her afterwards and began dealing with her regarding her need to be saved. He showed her Bible verses about sin and then asked her if she knew what sin was. She replied, "Selling drugs?" Obviously, it was something she had observed taking place in her home.

The worker affirmed that selling drugs certainly was a sin, but then he showed her Revelation 21:8. As he read, "...and all liars, shall have their part in the lake which burneth with fire and brimstone: which is the second death," she had a look on her face not only of guilt but of fear. The Holy Spirit through His Word was working on that nine-year-old girl's heart. She realized that sin was not just what grown-ups did but that she was also a sinner and needed to be saved. In a few minutes she bowed her head and trusted Christ as her personal Saviour. That is the spiritual work that we want.

Here are some simple suggestions to keep your work in the bus ministry on a spiritual level of faith.

1. Acknowledge that you are doing God's work and tell Him you are depending on Him as you work. Never do anything in your own power or for your own purpose. Let the Lord know that you know you need Him

- ◆ to lead you to the right people;
- ◆ to give you the right words to say;
- ◆ to make the right decisions.

2. Lead your workers to do their work by faith in God. Remind them often that this work is of the Lord, for the Lord, and cannot be blessed without the Lord. We need Him if we are to have fruit that remains. We must not attempt a spiritual work in our own strength and power. For every part of the work we must rely on God

- ◆ for wisdom,
- ◆ for strength,
- ◆ for the filling of the Holy Spirit,
- ◆ for love.

3. Begin your day and work in the bus ministry in prayer.

- Pray for God's blessings on your work.
- Pray for God to bless and use your workers.
- Pray for those you visit.
- Pray for souls to be saved.

4. Pray throughout the day of work. Never stop relying on God for His blessings and for the increase to your labors

- as you drive the bus to pick up the riders,
- as you run your program,
- as you teach and preach,
- as you visit your riders.

5. Teach your riders the importance of having faith in God. The greatest way to teach this is to remind them of how God is working in their lives. In everything, point them to the Lord.

- When they have a need, pray with them and remind them to trust the Lord.
- When they receive a blessing, remind them to give praise to the Lord.
- When they are burdened, remind them that God loves them and cares about them.

Faith is remembering that the things we see are brought about by things we cannot see. America was founded on this truth, yet today it is being undermined. Everything that pleases God is under attack. If we attempt to fix a spiritual problem without supernatural means, we will fail every time. The only way we can accomplish a true work of God is by faith. Let us do our work in the bus ministry not by habit, but by faith in Him.

Taking It to the Next Level

MANY churches look back over the years of being in the bus ministry with a warmth and excitement as they see the amazing things God has done in the lives of so many.

- ◆ Families faithfully attend church who were reached through the bus ministry.

- ◆ Men who grew up in the bus ministry serve as deacons, and other men and women who were reached through the bus ministry now teach Sunday school classes or work bus routes.

- ◆ Teens are actively involved in the youth program and serving the Lord.

- ◆ Young adults are in Christian college preparing for a life in ministry.

- ◆ Some even serve in full-time Christian service as pastors, bus directors, Christian school teachers, or in other capacities.

Why do others who get into the bus ministry never experience results such as these? What makes the difference? Let me first state that only eternity will reveal the true fruit of the efforts put forth on bus routes. There are churches that serve faithfully but do not enjoy the visible results that others do. Had we judged the earthly ministry of Christ by the number of people who stayed by His side all the way to the cross, we would have certainly deemed Him to have failed. Certainly we would have questioned His methods.

1. Persistence. Here is the bottom line. The church that stays faithful in a ministry the longest will experience the greatest and most lasting results. If you visited our church today, you might make the mistake of assuming that we have had some superphenomenal growth. Let me assure you that God has blessed, but our growth has averaged about one hundred per year. In other words, our church has not "mushroomed" because of the bus ministry; but, then, we are not in the bus ministry just for numbers. We are in it to win souls. Win souls and your church will grow.

Dr. Hyles wrote an article entitled "Where Are the Nine?" in which he said, "Soul winning is not a method of church building. It is a command from our Commanding General. Occasionally someone will come to the Pastors' School at First Baptist Church of Hammond, spend a week hearing and seeing the soul-winning emphasis here, and go home to win souls and see his church grow. This growth may continue for several years, and then it may level off. Often this same pastor will then go to someone else's pastors' school to find other methods by which he can build his attendance. Soul winning is not a method; it is a command. We are supposed to go soul winning and do soul winning if our churches grow or if our churches decrease in attendance. An increase in church attendance is simply a delightful product of soul winning; but if such an increase does not occur, the command of the Great Commission is no less valid."

That is exactly what I believe about the bus ministry. The end is not growth, but the by-product often is. The real "secret" is to do it for the right reason for a long period of time. Let God bless in His timing. Don't force growth. I did not say not to promote. Promotions are good, but do not make growth the main goal. Be persistent in what you believe and allow God to bring the increase.

2. Personal attention. This is a vital part of success. Every bus kid I have known who fully gave his life to the Lord is one who was given personal attention by a leader. Jesus gave personal attention to His disciples. They were often confused and doubtful, but He patiently taught them and brought them to a place where they committed themselves to Him. The same will be true on our bus routes. We must give personal attention if we want to have a greater influence on their lives.

3. Graded Sunday school. In the past I have heard of men who used the bus route to get people saved and baptized but then put them in a giant unified Sunday school/church assembly. Back in the '60s and '70s when there were so many growing churches using the methods of Dr. Hyles, some veered from what he taught and did not follow his plan of having a graded Sunday school. While he continued to operate a graded Sunday school for his bus kids, they went to the unified plan. Why did they do so?

◆ It required fewer workers.

◆ It took less time. They conducted just one service instead of having Sunday school and church.

◆ It was more space friendly—no need for little classrooms.

◆ It better fit with their Christian schools. Many began to build for their schools rather than their Sunday schools. They could use their gymnasiums to conduct a giant service.

While these sincere men were trying to do what they thought was best, they abandoned the principle that Dr. Hyles and others had taught and used for so long. They quit having long-term results, and as a result some lost faith in the bus ministry. Nothing can replace the effect of a small class Sunday school. There are ways to work around space issues which I cover elsewhere in this book.

4. Vibrant teen program. Children will grow up; and as they do, they will change along with their needs. If you do not provide a youth program to fit these needs, you will lose many of these young people. They will build their lives around something. We want them to build their lives around the church but must provide means for their doing so. I go into more detail in another chapter as to what we can do to keep the teens active and involved. Whatever you do, do not neglect to go to the next level with these young people.

5. Strong adult classes. This is a twofold proposition. First, we must provide a good Sunday school program for the adults reached through the bus ministry. Second, we must provide good Sunday school opportunities for the children as they become adults.

6. "Three to thrive." Dr. Lee Roberson was the one who made this slogan famous. He would often say in his inimitable voice, "It takes three to thrive—Sunday morning, Sunday night and Wednesday night." He was right, of course. If you want to go to the next level, you need to make it possible for many of these bus riders to get to church for more services. I am not suggesting that you must run buses every service. That would not be practical. However, we must do what we can to get some of our bus riders back on Sunday nights and if possible on Wednesday nights as well.

7. The Christian school. The question is whether or not this is practical or possible for many of our bus kids. Let's face it, the public schools are long gone as far as any semblance of Christian values remaining in them is concerned. Can we take the bus kids to the next level of Christian growth without getting them out of public school and into Christian school? The first answer is that we must. In most cases, it is impossible for us to find the means to get all these kids enrolled in our schools. Some churches have attempted to operate separate schools for these kids. Others have made efforts to enroll a few each year on a work scholarship plan. Many churches have worked to get a foothold in the public schools for Bible club programs and have used the bus kids to gain a foothold.

My answer to this issue is that we must by as many means as possible take these kids to the next level in any way we can, whether that be through the Christian school or through public school Bible clubs. Every church must do whatever they can.

Going to the next level requires a vision and a plan, and it will not happen overnight, but it will never happen if we do not see the need or make the effort.

The day will come when you watch your first bus kid receive his degree from a Christian college, perform your first wedding of a bus kid who grew up in your church, ordain to the gospel ministry a young man who rode your buses to Sunday school as a child, or dedicate the baby of a faithful young couple who once were bus kids. On any of those days you will experience the immense joy and pleasure of knowing you did what you could to make a difference in their lives. It can happen for you, but first you must decide to take it to the next level.

STARTING A NEW
BUS ROUTE

BIRTH brings new life. Churches with new converts are exciting and alive. Sunday school classes with new attendees stay fresh and alive. The same is true about the bus ministry. Maintaining what you have can bring on complacency, while expansion stirs up great energy and excitement. For that reason I believe that a church should always be looking toward starting new routes.

When first starting a bus ministry, you obviously will be starting new routes. However, perhaps you are expanding your current bus ministry and want to start a new route or two. Over the years I have had plenty of experience at this, and there are several important principles that I believe will help you with this exciting venture.

1. Set the date. Starting a new route should be exciting and akin to planting a new church. For that reason I recommend that you set a date several weeks out and begin letting everyone know what your plans are.

- ◆ Plan your kickoff to coincide with your fall or spring program.
- ◆ Visit in the area for several weeks before the launch date.
- ◆ Enjoy the process. The days getting ready for a new church or new route are exciting days.

2. Decide on the area. This is of utmost importance. Boundaries are important especially if your routes are close to one another. You do not want there to be a "territory war" among routes. Often a new route will overlap with an established one, so decide if the riders will ride on their present route or be a part of the new one. Here are some things to consider when choosing an area for a new route.

- Lower- to middle-class neighborhoods
- Nearby apartments or trailer parks
- Neighborhood schools
- Distance from church: Is it reasonable?
- Safety of the neighborhood: Be careful about putting your workers in potentially dangerous situations:
- Potential to build: Be sure the area can support a bus route.
- Kids in the area: If the mobile homes are senior housing, a bus route may not be the right method for reaching that area.

3. Enlist the workers. Obviously, you must find the right people to work your new route. I recommend that the workers for new routes be chosen from people who are already working on other routes and that they be replaced on their former routes with new workers.

- Always be grooming new captains. When you see the potential in a bus worker to be a captain, begin preparing him and making certain he is ready.
- Sell the vision to all your captains so they will not resent one of their workers' moving to the new route. The entire bus ministry should feel they have a part in starting this route.
- Replace the workers who are moving to the new route with fresh, new workers. Losing a worker to a new route can actually be a good way to interject some fresh, new ideas into an existing route.
- Do not overextend your routes. Make certain you have plenty of workers in place to cover the existing routes as well as the new one.

4. Involve the church. There should be an excitement throughout the church as you wait and prepare for the new route to start. Churches that involve the entire congregation in these things always get behind the new route in a greater way.

◆ Ask people who are not bus workers to help visit in the area.

◆ Take a special offering to buy a new bus for that route.

◆ Send your soul winners to knock on doors.

◆ Introduce the workers on the new route to the church the Sunday night before.

◆ The Sunday the route starts, in your evening service, let the church know how it went.

5. Get everything in order. Make sure you have a nice, clean bus for them. A new route should be like a couple preparing for a new baby. Everything should be in place before the baby is born. Make certain you get everything ready for your new route.

◆ Equipment, including the bus and the things relating to it

◆ Workers

◆ Extra fliers

◆ Forms and other materials

6. Prepare the church for the new attendees. Remember there are others who will be affected by the new bus route. A new bus route means more people using your facilities. Think in advance of the things that will possibly be affected by a new route.

◆ Greeters

◆ Sunday school departments and classes

◆ Baptism workers

◆ Janitorial crew: You may need more chairs set up.

◆ Children's church workers

◆ Office staff: You will need more forms and fliers.

7. Have an extra-special promotion for the kick-off Sunday. Use something that has been hugely effective in the past. A good promotion will be a great help for the workers to get more children to ride the bus on the very first Sunday. Planning for the first day of a new route to coincide with a big day can be very effective.

8. Be spiritually prepared. With all the planning that goes into making certain you are ready for the beginning of a new route, do not forget the most important elements which are the spiritual ones. You need God's power and presence as you launch into this new venture. Without Him, all your work and efforts will be for naught.

- ◆ Pray.
- ◆ Make sure your heart is right.
- ◆ Pray some more.
- ◆ Ask others to pray.

So now you should be ready to start that new route. I trust hundreds of routes will be successfully launched, bringing untold numbers of boys and girls as well as their families to the Lord as a result.

MUSIC ON THE BUS

THERE are two things that affect morality more than most anything else. One is fashion, or dress. The other is music. Music plays a vital role in our culture and society. In fact, I do not know of anything where music does not have some influence. Music is all around us. It is everywhere you go. It is in the grocery store, the department stores, the mall, at sporting events, and almost everywhere else we go. Sadly, most of the music is not Christ honoring. Because music not only affects our minds but also "sticks" in them, it is one of the main tools the Devil uses to advance sin of every kind.

Music is also a vital part of the Christian life. We praise the Lord with music. Music allows us to express our heart and love for the Lord Jesus. Music teaches doctrine and truth. I love Christ-honoring music.

Most of us remember songs that we wish we could forget. It is amazing how a tune or a statement can bring to our memories a worldly song from the past.

Music is also an important tool for ministering to those who ride our buses to church. A successful bus route is one that uses music effectively, so it is important that we know the right way to use music. Here are some ideas.

1. Use Scripture songs. Can you think of anything that accomplishes more than singing the actual words of the Bible? The Bible tells us to hide God's Word in our hearts so we won't sin against Him. Singing is a great way to hide, embed, the Word of God in our hearts. It is so good to learn and sing songs that are the very words of our Lord in the Bible. By the way, it is the best memorization method that I have ever known. We need to use music and singing in a positive manner to learn the words of God.

2. Be sure the tune and the words are Christ honoring. You do not need to use worldly or contemporary songs to appeal to your bus kids. They need to learn the right kind of songs. Some bus workers use worldly songs or use music in an improper manner. The purpose of singing is more than having fun. Do not use songs that are nothing more than an excuse for a tune. That is the pattern of the contemporary church today. We do not want to follow that pattern; we want to use music that honors Christ. Sing with the right purpose in mind.

- We sing to praise God.
- We sing to hide truths in the children's hearts.
- We sing to teach doctrine.
- We sing to teach Scripture.

3. Do not allow the culture of the world to change our music. Some bus routes have added a "rap type" music to Christian music. We should not allow the culture of our day to affect our work for Christ, but our work for Christ should affect the culture of the day. Teach the children why we sing Christian songs and why we use music that honors the Lord and why we don't use that which dishonors Him.

It is a blessing to hear of parents and grandparents of these children speaking of the songs we have taught their kids. One young lady told me that she went to her grandparents' house one evening and sang the songs that she learned on the bus route. They asked her to sing them over and over again because they enjoyed them so much. They were so proud of her.

The story did not end there. That young lady asked her grandparents if they had ever received Christ as their Saviour. They had not, so she took a church tract and led them to Christ. It all started when she sang those songs from the bus route.

4. Have fun with music. Music can be fun without being

worldly or carnal. Songs with motions are favorites. Someone said, "Motion creates emotion." I am inclined to believe that to be true. We can have fun without the sinfulness of the world! The following good old songs have a tremendous spiritual meaning but are fun as well. All the workers should participate (with the exception of the bus driver, of course) in singing and the motions. Children love to sing motion songs, and there are some wonderful songs children enjoy singing.

◆ Deep and Wide
◆ He's Able
◆ I'm in the Lord's Army
◆ Away Far Over Jordan

5. **Repeat songs over and over again.** We all love to sing our favorites songs over and over again. Children love to sing songs they know. My wife and I have five children. Throughout the years we had certain songs that we sang probably hundreds of times with our children. They never tired of singing the same songs over and over. While we need to teach them as many good new songs as possible, we need not shy away from singing the good old ones often. Never stop singing songs like "Jesus Loves Me," "The B-I-B-L-E" and others we learned in our childhood.

6. **Sing songs that teach character.** There are many good songs that can help instill biblical values and Christian character into children. It is good to place these in their minds and allow them to be there throughout the week in a world that teaches opposite values. Find good songs that accomplish this purpose and use them over and over again—songs about obedience, honesty, purity, and dedication.

7. **Sing songs about Jesus.** There are so many great songs; but in thinking back to your own childhood, what was the song that you remember the most? I wouldn't be surprised if you answered "Jesus Loves Me." The songs of our childhood had a profound influence on all of us that endures until today. Give your bus kids the joy of singing good songs that replace the garbage songs of this world. Remember your days as a child and share these great

songs with others even now as you sing,

> **Jesus loves me! This I know,**
> **For the Bible tells me so.**
> **Little ones to Him belong;**
> **They are weak, but He is strong.**
>
> **Yes, Jesus loves me!**
> **Yes, Jesus loves me!**
> **Yes, Jesus loves me!**
> **The Bible tells me so.**

Now wasn't that a blessing?

THE BUSES

IT WOULDN'T be a bus ministry without buses, so we need to discuss this important element. More questions about buses come to me than about almost any other aspect of the bus ministry.

- Where can I find buses?
- Should I buy or lease them?
- Should I buy them new or used?
- Should I have a bus garage and a full-time mechanic on staff?

There are basically two elements regarding buses. The first is the procuring of the buses. The second is regarding maintenance and upkeep. Let me begin with a very simple outline of my philosophy regarding procuring buses. It is not the only one, and I would not fight over this. However, the Lord has privileged me to be involved in the bus ministry for many years, and this is what has worked best in our ministry.

1. I prefer to buy buses. There are few ministries who have the ability to lease buses and few ministries to whom buses are available for lease. The school systems have gone so far in the "separation of church and state" that very few will actually lease their buses.

2. We buy our buses at local auctions. Obviously, we look for buses with low mileage that look good and appear to be mechanically sound, preferably not more than ten years old. The bus

director should be responsible for this. If he is not very good with engines, he should find a man in the church to help him with this.

3. We use a bus for three to four years or until it becomes too expensive to continue maintaining it. We then sell the older bus for scrap and buy more buses.

For the remainder of this chapter, I will cover the area of maintaining your buses. A good bus ministry will make certain the buses are safe and trustworthy. Preventive work is always the best because it will reduce the number of breakdowns.

1. **Do a weekly check of the buses.** I recommend that each driver fill out a bus report when the day is finished and before he leaves. You want to make certain that he reports immediately any problems with the bus.

- Check the fluids such as oil, water, power steering, transmission, etc.
- Check the tires.
- Check the windows.
- Check warning signals and buzzers.
- Check steps and handrails.
- Check for cleanliness.
- Check the fuel.
- Check the lights.
- Check the mirrors.
- Check the horn.
- Check fire extinguishers.
- Check for possible exhaust leaks.

2. **Perform seasonal checks on the buses.** This is important. The details of this vary from one geographical region to another. Some things to check:

- Antifreeze added for winter
- Heat valves turned on in winter and off in summer
- Air tanks drained
- Radiator covers on in winter and removed in summer

◆ Inside heater working in the winter

3. **Keep the cosmetic matters cared for regularly.**

◆ Seat covers repaired and foam replaced

◆ Stickers removed from windows

◆ Painted areas checked for any needed touchup jobs, and rust covered

◆ Exterior washed

◆ Inside cleaned: You may have gum to scrape off and even a bit of graffiti to remove or cover.

◆ Trash cans and brooms provided

4. **Annual matters.** There are several important areas of concern that should be a priority with your buses.

◆ A DOT inspection: Make certain the buses are well prepared for this inspection and that problems are fixed beforehand.

◆ An emissions test for vehicles under 10,000 pounds gross weight.

◆ Registration: Make certain your buses are kept up to date.

◆ Insurance: Is every bus on the policy, and is the policy updated?

◆ The need for new buses: On an annual basis make certain you decide if it is time for some buses to be scrapped and new ones to be purchased.

5. **Finances.** When you are drawing up your new budget for the coming year, make certain that enough money is set aside for the upkeep of the buses. You may be running more buses than you were last year and need to increase your budget amount for the upcoming year.

These are very basic guidelines but enough to give you guidance in the concerns you should have. Remember, your bus ministry is only going to be effective if your equipment is safe and trustworthy. It is a part of the ministry we must not neglect or take for granted.

FORMS AND RECORD KEEPING

D O NOt make the mistake of underestimating the importance of this chapter. I wish could find a way to illuminate this chapter so that every pastor and bus director would read and implement these principles. Forms and record keeping could be the area that one day saves your church from a serious lawsuit or even saves the life of a child.

- ◆ Take it seriously.
- ◆ Teach it to your workers.
- ◆ Enforce the use of these procedures.
- ◆ Update your records on a weekly basis.
- ◆ Be thorough.

All things in God's work should be done decently and in order, and without good records that will not happen the way it should. Here is why keeping good records is so important.

1. **It provides security for the children and their parents.** The Bible teaches us to care for the children, so we should care for our bus children as least as well as the public school would care for them. One way we do this is by keeping records of their attendance. Keeping good records ensures that a parent can know where his child is each Sunday.

2. **It provides security for the church.** As a local church we are representing Christ, so we must strive to stay above reproach.

Keeping good records will assist you if any legal accusation is made.

On occasion we have had parents call the church because they did not know where their child was. We were able to check the records to find out whether or not their child attended on any given day. It is possible that the child went to a friend's house without telling the parents. If the child were to come home hurt or scratched, the records would show that the child was not on the bus. We once had problems with some teenagers that rode the bus, and we were forced to call the police. When the police officer saw the care we took in keeping records on every child, he was amazed and cooperated completely with us.

3. It provides safety for the children. Keeping forms and attendance records ensures that if any emergency occurs, we have the telephone number and information needed to contact the parent immediately. Accidents happen occasionally, and if you have no way of informing the parents, you will possibly lose that child. Communication wards off many new problems and often makes existing ones less severe.

4. It helps you keep discipline on your bus. If every child knows that you have his parents' telephone number and that you have weekly contact with them, he will usually behave better. If the children know what their consequences are for misbehaving, they will usually behave better.

5. It helps in rewarding the kids. Keeping records for faithful attendance and for bringing their Bibles is a great way to motivate some children to ride the bus. You cannot reward faithfulness if you have not kept records. Record keeping is far more than a necessary evil to keep us out of trouble. It is also a positive way to build the bus route.

6. It is the only proper way to grow your bus route. If you do not keep records, you may forget about a child. When a visitor comes, make certain that all his information is recorded so that a follow-up visit can be made. Don't trust your memory. Keeping records for follow-up assures you that every child is visited weekly.

7. It allows another person to be a helper on the bus. The best secretary is not always the person who can sing the loudest or even work best with the children. Often it is someone who will

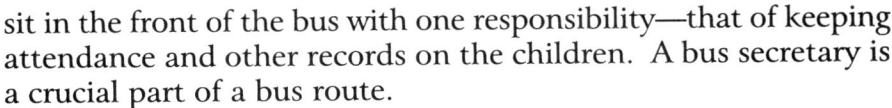

sit in the front of the bus with one responsibility—that of keeping attendance and other records on the children. A bus secretary is a crucial part of a bus route.

8. It gives you a guide to help you pray for the kids. Provide a list of all your bus children to each worker on your bus so that you can pray for them. We must wage a spiritual battle for our bus children. The Devil never stops attacking them; therefore, we must intercede for them in prayer throughout the week.

9. It gives you a guide in the event the bus captain is sick or out of town. Without record keeping, imagine what would happen if for some reason the captain was not available to visit or run the route on Sunday.

10. It helps you keep tabs on the faithfulness of the riders. Obviously, it is important to know how faithful your riders have been so that you can follow up with them faithfully. Keeping good records makes this possible. You can also keep records of other things that may be important to track.

- Date accepted Christ
- Date baptized
- Bible brought
- Visitors brought
- Scripture memorization

Be aware of these things as you organize your records and forms. Once you understand their importance, you will be more likely to get these implemented soon. We will discuss the forms and records in another chapter; but for now, be aware that without record keeping, you are wide open for problems that could be prevented.

THE FORMS AND RECORDS

IT HAS BEEN said that forms are seldom fun but usually functional. Churches without good forms and record-keeping systems are setting themselves up for problems. Some churches are very adept at using the latest technology to maintain all their records, but most still are probably not. If you can design a digital system that allows you to keep records for your bus ministry, that is great; but make certain that your records are:

- user- or worker-friendly—easily taught and learned;

- thorough—all information is important;

- accessible—if workers cannot access them, they are of little use;

- current—updated on a weekly basis.

Assuming that you are not anxious to reinvent the wheel, let me give you two record-keeping systems I recommend to pastors and bus directors for their bus ministries. The first system is the Dr. Beebe System, which uses the Universal attendance form (a). This form comes in triplicate or single form. It is used to sign up the children on Saturday visitation and also to keep attendance throughout the year. This form fits in a bus binder (b) or archboards (c). It is a proven system that many find simple and convenient.

The second system I recommend is the "four in one" form (d)

and the attendance book. This system uses a "four in one" form to sign up the riders on Saturday and to keep all their personal information. The attendance book is used on Sunday to keep attendance. The attendance book is designed for an entire year with 52 weeks of forms. These forms fit in the binder.

The reason this is called the "four in one" form is that it accomplishes four things with one form. This is used in conjunction with an attendance book that allows you to keep record of your attendance on a weekly basis (e).

◆ Gets the rider's personal information

◆ Obtains written permission from the parent for the child to ride the bus

◆ Presents the Gospel to the parents

◆ Obtains optional parental permission for baptism

Both of these systems work only as well as you will work them. Record keeping is not an easy job but is essential to operating a good bus route.

In addition to these, there is one other form that is required by law. The vehicle inspection log (f) insures that you could not get sued for negligence if you get into a wreck or breakdown. Every Sunday the bus driver must take a few minutes to fill out this form, or he could be fined/ticketed for failing to do so.

Whatever system you use, make certain you use it and allow it to make your ministry more organized and effective.

(a) Universal attendance form

(b) bus binder

(c) archboards

(d) "four in one" form

(e) attendance book

(f) vehicle inspection log

Each of these may be ordered from beebepublications.com .

MAINTAINING YOUR BUS

S OMETIMES I get so focused on the work that I allow a little detail to miss my attention. Certainly we all do. Bus workers have so many things to think about that it is easy to ignore or forget some "little" matters, yet it is often these details that make a huge difference in the success of our routes.

Dr. Hyles used to tell the story of Michelangelo. One day a visitor came to his studio in Florence and commented, "I can't see that you have made any progress since I was here last time."

Michelangelo answered, "Oh, yes, I have made much progress. Look carefully, and you will see that I have retouched this part and that I have polished that part."

"Yes," said the visitor, "but those are all trifles."

Michelangelo replied, "Trifles make perfection and perfection is no trifle."

Here I want to encourage us to look at the "trifles" or little things on our buses and make sure we are doing all we can to keep our buses maintained the way we should. Buses can get dirty or in disrepair quickly; and at times we can get so caught up in the work, we forget some of these little details. So maybe this is a good time to be reminded of a few important details or, as Michelangelo called them, trifles.

1. Keep them clean. We need to think like a mother would

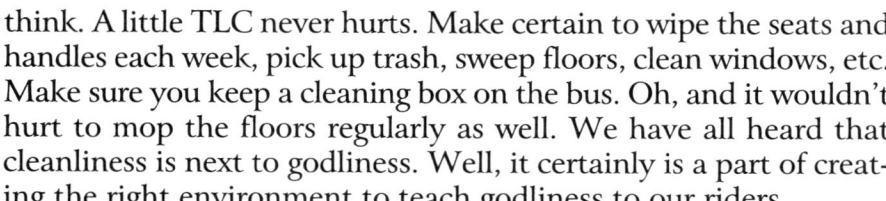
think. A little TLC never hurts. Make certain to wipe the seats and handles each week, pick up trash, sweep floors, clean windows, etc. Make sure you keep a cleaning box on the bus. Oh, and it wouldn't hurt to mop the floors regularly as well. We have all heard that cleanliness is next to godliness. Well, it certainly is a part of creating the right environment to teach godliness to our riders.

    2. Keep them sanitized. It is a good idea to keep some disinfectant wipes on the bus not only to make sure things are clean but that they are well sanitized. You also should make sure to have something to clean up potential accidents kids have from time to time. A couple of brown lunch bags can be useful when a child feels the need to throw up. Remember, cleanliness is not always just what we can see.

    3. Keep them attractive. A used bus may not be pretty, but we should do all we can to make our bus look as good as possible. A little touch-up of paint here or a little upholstery repair there can make a big difference in the pride of those on your bus. Make the bus look as nice as you can.

    4. Keep them repaired. Preventative maintenance is always best. Take a few minutes to make sure the oil and other fluid levels are good, the tires are good, the brakes are safe, all flashers and lights both inside and outside are operating properly, seats are bolted down and cushions are not loose, doors open and shut properly, entries are safe, emergency door is not blocked, etc. Guard the special lives that will ride that bus by being aware of the condition of your bus. Do not leave it to a mechanic to be the only one aware. You be aware as well. Report any problems immediately so they can be looked at and repaired.

    5. Keep them safe. Are there any sharp edges where a child could be injured? Are the steps safe? Are the guardrails secure? All of these are things we must not neglect or forget. Make sure to have a first aid kit with you as well and check it weekly to make sure all the supplies are there; **and**—do not forget to keep your workers aware of safety measures. Also, be sure you have an up-to-date fire extinguisher and that you know how to operate it if it is needed.

    6. Keep them fun. When the riders get on the bus, make sure there are posters with fun colors and things that make it more than just a bus. Make it a rolling classroom where they can learn the things of the Lord in an exciting atmosphere. Use streamers, balloons, posters, etc., to make the bus a fun place.

7. Keep them ready. Before that bus goes on the road, think of everything you may need to make it a successful Sunday. Have a checklist of all the things you need for all the activities planned and for as many as possible unforeseen potentialities. Go through it carefully and be sure you are always prepared. Proper preparation is a sign of love and care. It also prevents problems that could hinder the work of God in your riders.

Let's face it. We all get comfortable in our environment, and that can sometimes lead to carelessness. The longer we go without problems, the less likely we are to prepare properly for them. Treat each Sunday with the same seriousness you would if the riders on that route were your own children and family. Bus worker, don't neglect the trifles.

THE IMPORTANCE OF
A GOOD EXAMPLE

"In all things shewing thyself a pattern of good works: in doctrine shewing uncorruptness, gravity, sincerity,

"Sound speech, that cannot be condemned; that he that is of the contrary part may be ashamed, having no evil thing to say of you."—Titus 2:7, 8.

WHAT IS the most important aspect of the bus ministry in the lives of children and teenagers? Is it the program on the bus? Is it the Bible teaching in Sunday school? Is it the preaching of the Word in church? Without a doubt, these are all very important aspects. However, perhaps the most important one of all is the opportunity to give these children a living example of what the Christian life is all about. For most of them, it is the only example they may ever have. We are all concerned as to what will happen to America if character and moral behavior continue to decline in our children. There are so few examples of godliness in our world today. Where will that be corrected if not through the church?

Children are looking for an example or a pattern to follow in their lives. The question is whether that example will be a good one or a bad one. There is a desire within all of us to emulate others. Bus children often have a desire to follow a sports star or a musician of some kind.

- ◆ They copy what they wear.

- ◆ They copy their speech and music.
- ◆ They copy their lifestyles.
- ◆ Sadly, they even copy their values.

We lose our children to these wicked examples, while most of them have no alternative examples in their lives to copy. We must become that alternative. There are young people in our cities and towns who are looking for a different kind of example to copy and to follow. We must become their example.

We cannot compete with the mass appeal of these poor examples, but there must be a place where the children can find a good pattern to copy. That is the church; and for many, that begins with the bus workers. It may surprise all of us if we knew how many children do copy or emulate the life of a bus captain. Often parents have told me, "That boy of mine will get in his room with a Bible and preach up a storm," or, "Our children act out the bus program when they are at home playing. They sing the songs and tell the Bible stories." What are these kids doing? They are copying the bus captain and workers. Many parents even tell us they are thankful for the good example being provided by those workers.

A pattern is something that is intended to be copied. It must be clear and simple so that it can be copied. Noah Webster's 1828 dictionary defines *pattern:* "an original or model proposed for imitation; the archetype; that which is to be copied or imitated, either in things or in actions; as the pattern of a machine; a pattern of patience." Noah Webster often used the Bible for examples. He said: "Christ was the most perfect pattern of rectitude, patience and submission ever exhibited on earth."

> **Note:** Too many preachers today use secular dictionaries to define Bible terms rather than using the Bible to define Bible words!

The word "pattern" is a commonly used word in the Bible.

"And let them make me a sanctuary; that I may dwell among them.

"According to all that I shew thee, after the pattern of the tabernacle, and the pattern of all the instruments thereof, even so

shall ye make it."—Exod. 25:8, 9.

"Then David gave to Solomon his son the pattern of the porch, and of the houses thereof, and of the treasuries thereof, and of the upper chambers thereof, and of the inner parlours thereof, and of the place of the mercy seat."—I Chron. 28:11.

"Let no man despise thy youth; but be thou an example [or pattern] *of the believers, in word, in conversation, in charity, in spirit, in faith, in purity."*—I Tim. 4:12.

Our lives are to be a pattern that can be copied and followed by those whom we reach in the bus ministry. Here are some areas where we need to be a pattern for our bus riders. Look at the things Paul said to Timothy and become that example to your bus kids.

1. A pattern in word or kindness. We should not yell or express anger when we are with our bus riders. It is important to express kindness in every way. Think about being kind. Use kind expressions. Perform kind gestures and actions.

"And be ye kind one to another, tenderhearted, forgiving one another, even as God for Christ's sake hath forgiven you."—Eph. 4:32.

2. A pattern in conversation or our responses to others. Perhaps the most difficult behavior to control is our response to others when they have been unkind to us or have treated us wrongly. Only a Spirit-filled Christian can show forth the example we should be. Let me challenge you to claim the power of the Holy Spirit and to respond in a kind and righteous manner when dealing with difficult situations.

"Dearly beloved, avenge not yourselves, but rather give place unto wrath: for it is written, Vengeance is mine; I will repay, saith the Lord."—Rom. 12:19.

These young people typically see only a pattern of hatefulness and a vengeful response in their world. The Bible teaches us to respond differently.

"A soft answer turneth away wrath: but grievous words stir up anger."—Prov. 15:1.

3. A pattern of charity or love. These children have learned all about lust, but few have seen real love in action. Our example in love is in direct contrast to the constant barrage of lies Satan tells them about fleshly love, which is most often driven by lust. Pure love is a lesson they can learn by example as you show them the pure, giving love of Christ.

"A new commandment I give unto you, That ye love one another; as I have loved you, that ye also love one another."—John 13:34.

4. A pattern of spirit or attitude. Are you an example of consistency in the way you behave? Are you one who shows forth a positive joy in your life?

"Then he said unto them, Go your way, eat the fat, and drink the sweet, and send portions unto them for whom nothing is prepared: for this day is holy unto our Lord: neither be ye sorry; for the joy of the LORD is your strength."—Neh. 8:10.

These kids see so much despair and negativity. That drains us all. They step on that bus, and suddenly they are strengthened by the spirit on the bus. They go home happy and joyful. Their parents see that and wonder why. The influences of the world make those same kids sullen, but church makes them joyful. A great way to change lives is by the example we set in our spirits.

5. A pattern of faith. Never forget that these kids go back into the same world that has influenced them up to this point. Are we setting a good example of showing them how to trust the Lord?

"Trust in the LORD with all thine heart; and lean not unto thine own understanding."—Prov. 3:5.

Our challenges, our struggles and our suffering are often God's way of testing our faith as well as allowing us to be an example to others. These kids watch you. You will have times when you face opportunities to trust God too. As the children watch, are you setting a good example for them?

6. A pattern of godliness in modest dress. With all of the heathen examples of dress promoted in stores and on television, it is difficult for our children to comprehend modest or decent dress. You may be the only pattern of decency they will see. It is important for them to see Christians dressed in Christ-honoring clothes when they come to church.

"As obedient children, not fashioning yourselves according to the former lusts in your ignorance."—I Pet. 1:14.

Some criticize the emphasis we place on dress, but do you realize that fashion drives morality? I am amazed how the world knows this and we miss it. Dress leads to the loosening of standards of morality in people's lives. Is it any surprise that the way we dress is influenced so predominantly by the most immoral of society? They control the way we dress and in essence control the way we live.

This is a big deal, and we should make it a big deal on our bus routes. Bus captain, they are watching you. They love and admire you, and they want to be like you. Set the right example. Be the godly pattern they so desperately need. Be the Christian that they would do well to emulate.

THE HEART OF
A CHILD

"Foolishness is bound in the heart of a child; but the rod of correction shall drive it far from him."—Prov. 22:15.

WHAT IS IN the heart of every child? What makes him tick? The Bible tells us that within the confines of every child's heart resides foolishness. *Foolishness* is defined as "the trait of acting stupidly or rashly." Watch children as they play or interact. They do rash things or things that we as adults would consider to be stupid or foolhardy. They play with reckless abandonment, often with no care of potential danger. A child will run out into the street with no thought of the danger involved.

Does that mean that children are born evil? I believe that they are born sinners but not evil. It is their sin that condemns their soul, but it is their foolishness that destroys their lives. A criminal is a person who did not have the foolishness 'driven far from him.' Where there is no parental rod, there often comes a legal rod to replace it. The law punishes that one whose parents did not correct him. We live in a society where the foolishness of children is laughed at and even carried on well into adulthood. That has left us with irresponsible adults who act rashly or on impulse rather than with self-control.

The bus ministry is one place where we become involved with many children who behave foolishly. Do not assume that these children are horrible because of their foolish behavior. They were born with it bound in their hearts.

◆ The foolish behavior of a child does not start out as evil. It may become evil if he is influenced by evil and not corrected of his foolishness.

◆ Foolish behavior does not start out as hateful behavior unless in his folly he is surrounded by hateful or unloving people.

◆ Foolish behavior does not start out as violent behavior unless the foolish one is fed a steady diet of violence without reproof.

◆ Again, foolish behavior does not start out as deviant behavior unless the child has been subjected to deviant activities and influences with no correction being applied.

In many ways the bus ministry is where we interact with children who are often left uncorrected and we try to prevent them from destroying their lives. Many children never know the God-like love of parents who correct their foolishness. It is too inconvenient to the parents to discipline their children, or they are merely too busy. Often they don't even notice their children's foolishness because they are not involved in their lives. We come along not as parents but as servants of the Lord with a goal of claiming their lives for the Lord.

A bus worker is one who must know the hearts of those children who ride the bus and must understand what causes them to behave the way they do. Don't condemn them as bad apples when in truth their problem is that uncorrected foolishness is bound in their young hearts.

1. Children need correction. I contend that they want it. Correction is how we drive foolishness from their hearts. We bring these kids to church, and many of them get saved at a very young age. That does not correct the foolishness in their hearts. However, it does give us a powerful advantage because of the Spirit of God who then lives within them. Salvation will not remove the foolishness, but it may soften the cords that bind the foolishness in their hearts. Not all punishment is correction, but correction often leads to corrective punishment.

2. We cannot use the rod per se, but we must use strength. The rod represents authority. In this context, it represents more than just spanking; it stands for strength or authority. When we correct the children on the bus, we are giving them the chance to have a good life. These children have often seen the weakness of authority figures who are controlled by their own impulses. Brute force has been the way with which they have been handled all their lives. Punishment is not defined by their actions but by their parents' reactions. That has built up fear and resentment as well as confusion. What irritates Mom is fine with Dad. Wrong becomes situational rather than principled.

As Christian leaders we must replace that reactive weakness with corrective strength. We must make certain that all workers are on the same page when it comes to the rules and consequences of breaking those rules. One worker cannot wink at what another worker prohibits.

3. Without love, our correction is merely punishment. Punishment does in anger what correction does in love. Children who resist correction often do so because they have never known loving correction at home. The Bible tells us that the Lord only chastens those He loves as His own children. He loves us all, but He only chastens those in the family. If we are to have an influence on these kids' lives, we must correct them with the same kind of love we would have for our own children.

4. Bus routes must be under control. There must be discipline. There must be a system of rules and consequences. By teaching these children how to live in a world of rules, we are teaching them how to obey, which is paramount to the Christian life. By enforcing the consequences of violating the rules, we are teaching them that there is a price to pay for doing wrong, or for sin. If the goal were merely to get more people to church, then insisting on obedience would not matter. That is not the goal. The goal is to see lives changed for the glory of the Lord. We therefore must not merely maintain a certain level of "crowd control" but must teach these children the principles behind our correction.

5. Discipleship without discipline is impossible. Peter was an adult who was out of control. He took out his sword and reacted by cutting off the ear of the high priest's servant. That is interesting. Peter was a bit childish in his behavior at times. Patiently the Lord corrected him until Peter was discipled or disciplined enough to be used of the Lord in a greater way.

That is what we do with these young lives on our bus routes. We provide discipline in order to disciple them, not for our convenience but in order for their lives to be used for the Lord. See discipline not as a way to control your bus crowd but as a way to disciple your riders.

6. To be effective in correction, you must possess the fruits of the Spirit. If you look at the list of the fruits of the Spirit, you will find that each one is vital as we work with these young lives. These fruit are not for our enjoyment but for our effectiveness in living for others. These are to make us better spouses, parents, friends, neighbors, employees, preachers, teachers, bus workers, and servants of the Lord. They are qualities we should possess not for the enjoyment to ourselves but for the good of those around us.

"But the fruit of the Spirit is love, joy, peace, longsuffering, gentleness, goodness, faith,

"Meekness, temperance: against such there is no law."— Gal. 5:22, 23.

Think of your home and the way you deal with your own children. Then consider how Jesus practiced each of these fruits of the Spirit with His disciples. We are to be that in the way we deal with the children who ride our buses. When you correct with these qualities, you reap them in those you correct. We must know that in our flesh we will fail, but in His Spirit we will successfully reach these children and correct them from their foolishness.

Are some children born as "bad apples"? Are some hopelessly evil and thus unreachable? I believe not. I do believe that the longer the foolishness is bound in their hearts, the more evil can affect and infect them. Foolishness is like vulnerability. It is in every child, but as leaders we must do all we can to correct them and see to it that foolishness is driven far from them so that they can live prosperous lives for the Lord.

IV

THE
PROMOTIONS
AND VISITATION
OF THE BUS MINISTRY

GOAL SETTING, FULFILLING GOD'S PURPOSE

IN THE next two chapters I am going to deal with a subject that garners much debate, even criticism. Goal setting is often associated with "success gurus" and thus is criticized by well-meaning Christians. If my mind-set were to make a name for myself, then I would consider the criticism of my goal setting to be justifiable. However, I am not speaking of goals as a mere tool for success but rather as a tool of obedience. I believe in setting goals, and I believe that those who misunderstand my emphasis on goal setting do so because they do not understand my perspective.

Every year, I ask the individuals on my staff to present to me a review of their ministry or ministries. I ask them to provide three things to me.

1. A stated purpose of their ministry

2. A specific goal to accomplish that purpose

3. A detailed plan they will implement to accomplish that goal

Each staff member presents these to me so that I know what he is working towards within his area of responsibility. The plan is not first, nor is the goal. Everything follows the purpose. I refuse to apologize for setting goals, but I do believe that the principles in this chapter will help others better to recognize why I believe so strongly in setting goals. In order to understand the setting of goals, we must deal with these three principles.

1. We must first know our purpose. This is where it begins. Our purpose will determine our goals.

Let me give you an example. Jesus came to earth in the form of a man with specific purposes in mind. The Bible tells us exactly what these were.

"For the Son of man is come to seek and to save that which was lost."—Luke 19:10.

"Jesus saith unto them, My meat is to do the will of him that sent me, and to finish his work."—John 4:34.

1. To seek and to save that which was lost

2. To fulfill the law and do the will of the Father

Along the way there were other things that made up the completion of these two purposes. Jesus knew His purpose before He came, and everything He did along the way was in preparation for and fulfillment of those things.

Likewise, we are here for a purpose. Our purpose as Christians and within the church is given to us in God's Word.

"And he said unto them, Go ye into all the world, and preach the gospel to every creature."—Mark 16:15.

Jesus has commanded us to do something. He has defined our purpose for us.

1. He has told us to go into all the world.

2. He told us to preach the Gospel to every creature.

There is no doubt in my mind that the main purpose of the local church is not the exposition of the Word of God. It is to preach the Gospel to every creature. Now before you rip into me, I did not say that we should not teach the Bible in the church. That is part of the fulfillment of the Great Commission; so, yes, we should teach the Bible. However, even that must take us back to the main purpose which is to preach the Gospel to every creature. The problem in many churches today is that they are enamored by things other than the main purpose.

2. We must next set our goals. A goal is something that we establish in order that we might fulfill our purpose. Once we know our purpose, we must establish goals to fulfill that purpose. Then we must decide on a plan of action to accomplish those goals in order to fulfill that purpose. A goal without a plan is a wish.

Many churches do not reach their main purpose because they never establish goals nor devise a plan. A pastor who denies the importance of goals is depriving his people of the excitement of thriving by pursuing the bigger purpose.

The fact is that we all set some goals in our ministry. Show me your goals, and I will probably see your purpose. We must make certain that our goals reflect the purpose for our church and ministry. Here are some goals pastors often set.

- How many students we want to have in our Christian school
- How many missionaries we are going to support for the next year
- How much money we want to receive in offerings weekly
- How much money we want to raise for a special project
- How many Thanksgiving baskets we want to distribute
- How many basketball games we want our high school to schedule
- How many families we want to help at Christmastime
- How many churches we want to plant
- How many missions trips we want to take and how many we want to go on these trips
- How many boxes of candy we want to sell to raise funds for our school this year

These are good goals in our minds, and I would not necessarily disagree with them. However, I believe that we should take our goal setting even further.

- How many souls we want to see saved this year
- How many souls we want to see saved on a special Sunday
- How many baptisms we want during the next year
- How many we want to average in Sunday school in the fall or spring program

◆ How many we want to have attending Sunday school and church on a special-promotion Sunday

◆ How many riders a bus route wants to have on their big day

Why would it be acceptable to set a goal for money to be raised for missions but not for visitors on a big day? I will tell you why. It is because we have listened to critics of men like Dr. Beebe and Dr. Hyles who judged their motives without knowing their hearts. They told us that all they wanted was power or prestige, when in truth those who knew them understood that they did what they did in order to fulfill their purpose of preaching the Gospel to every creature.

Let me give you another example. I decided that as a part of fulfilling God's purpose for my life, I wanted to start local churches throughout the Allegheny mountain region as well as throughout my state of Kentucky. I set a goal of the number of churches I wanted to help start. Praise the Lord, as of this writing we have started twenty-two churches.

I could sit back and tell myself that I have done enough, but the purpose is still before me. The purpose never changes, but the goals do. As a result, I have increased my goal of the number of churches I want to help start.

Some men who would criticize my goal setting in attendance would praise my goal setting in church planting. I have goals for the number of missionaries I want to send to the foreign field. Likewise, I have goals for the number of souls I want to see won to Christ and the number of baptisms I want to see.

◆ Goals show me my progress.

◆ Goals test commitment.

◆ Goals keep me focused.

◆ Goals make me do more and want to do more.

We need to return to the excitement and results of the churches in the '60s and '70s. Some say that these churches fell because they were too enamored with numbers. I say that they failed because they lost sight of their purpose. The men who failed using Dr. Hyles' methods must have at some point stopped using his methods. He did not stop working those methods; and as a result, he did not stop growing.

3. Finally, we must establish and implement a plan. Jesus was a good planner. He knew where He was going before He went there, and He sent men to prepare for His coming.

> *"After these things the Lord appointed other seventy also, and sent them two and two before his face into every city and place, whither he himself would come.*
>
> *"Therefore said he unto them, The harvest truly is great, but the labourers are few: pray ye therefore the Lord of the harvest, that he would send forth labourers into his harvest."*—Luke 10:1, 2.

Sounds like a plan to me; and it sounds like He had a goal to go to at least thirty-five cities, assuming they went to only one city per team. In fact, each team may have gone to multiple cities. Doing what? Carrying out His plan. Jesus always had a plan, but we often miss it because good plans go off seamlessly. To say that He did not have a plan is to say that He just walked about "winging it," like many of us do with our soul winning. If He had thirty-five advance teams, then it is pretty obvious He knew where He was going.

Even in seeing His plan, we recognize His purpose. He spoke of the harvest and the need for laborers who would go into the harvest. His purpose was to seek and to save that which was lost. Is it not interesting that He never spoke of His purpose as being anything other than this?

"And he must needs go through Samaria."—John 4:4.

Why did Jesus **need** to go through Samaria? It was because He had an appointment with a lady in Sychar where He planned to preach to the entire city. He had a scheduled meeting with her at a well. She was going to do His advance work and bring the entire city to hear Him preach. He had a plan already in mind when He went.

I know, I know—you think that He anticipated this because He was God Incarnate. Wait, my friend, because He also told us that He was sending us to do the exact same thing His Father had sent Him to do.

"Then said Jesus to them again, Peace be unto you: as my Father hath sent me, even so send I you."—John 20:21.

I am to do what Jesus did with the same purpose of seeking the lost and leading them to Him. We know our purpose. Now we must set goals to accomplish that purpose in the greatest way possible. Then we must make our plans so that we can reach those goals. Do not think that Jeff Fugate is delusional. I know Satan hates soul winning and he does everything he can to disparage our methods and discourage our spirits. I plan to keep on setting goals so that I can do everything possible to fulfill my purpose of winning this world to Christ. Will you join me?

JUMP-STARTING YOUR BUS MINISTRY

O CCASIONALLY a pastor or bus director will approach me and ask how he can get his bus ministry moving again. He is frustrated because he senses that it has become stagnant, and he wants to try to get it going strong again.

A bus ministry, like any other ministry, will not stay successful unless leadership gives it the attention it needs. Anything left to itself will eventually experience failure. I believe that any ministry we leave to itself will also eventually fail. A ministry not properly organized and monitored can slip into disrepair.

Unfortunately, some bus ministries get treated like "a red-haired stepchild" by the pastors, and as a result the church members do not take them seriously. Perhaps this has happened to your bus ministry, however unintentional; but you must take inventory and decide if your bus ministry is faltering a bit. Maybe you thought you were doing the right things, but you still sense that it has lost steam. If so, perhaps all you need is a jump-start. Here are some things that have successfully been done by others that could perhaps help you to get it back on track.

1. **Do a check on your "want to."** Are you in the bus ministry because you really want to be or because you feel you have to be? Do you get excited about it, or is it a drain on you? You may be doing the basics right but still failing overall. We can have the "how to" down; but if we are weak in the "want to," our bus ministry

will suffer. As important as it is to do the right things, if we do not match that with our desire, we will experience failure. So what can you do to get the "want to" back?

◆ Listen to preaching that rekindles your burden for lost souls. That is what the bus ministry is all about. I do this often in order to keep my heart excited. Keeping a burden for the bus ministry is important to me.

◆ Fellowship with those who are passionate about the bus ministry. Let their passion and love rub off on you. You will not be around me for long without feeling my passion for this ministry. If you associate with preachers who are negative about the bus ministry, you will become negative as well.

◆ Read books and articles about the bus ministry that share testimonies and success stories. I hope you read the *Church Bus News.* I recommend you get every worker to subscribe and read every issue.

◆ Pray for God to rekindle the passion you once had. Drive around your bus neighborhoods and ask God to give you a burden for those children and families who need to hear about Christ.

◆ Remember the blessings of the past. I often think about the many souls who have been saved in these years of service. I think of those who are now in Heaven because of the bus ministry, some of whom were children. I look at pictures of children we have reached and think of how their lives have been transformed because someone in our bus ministry picked them up on a bus every Sunday and brought them to church.

The bus ministry will bring you challenges like no other ministry. Satan will attack it more than most other ministries because he knows its effectiveness in molding precious young lives for Christ. He hates that. A "want to" will make the difference in dealing with these attacks and problems. Without it, you may decide it is not worth the effort or cost.

If you look at any endeavor in life, you will discover difficulties and challenges. Think of the challenges attached to many things you love doing like hunting or fishing. You approach those challenges with great energy because you have the "want to." Russell Anderson, a Christian businessman who has given more than thirty million dollars to the Lord's work, says that a willingness to solve problems with a positive attitude was a great big key to his success in business. Apply that truth and see if it does not help jump-start your bus ministry.

2. Find new leaders. In most churches there are more people who want to serve the Lord than there are those who actually are serving Him. Many do not know where or how to serve. They will not admit it because they may think they can't do it. Perhaps no one has ever reached out to them and made them believe they are capable of doing a work for God. A great bus ministry is the result of a pastor or bus director who finds unlikely people and guides them to become great workers.

> **Note:** Finding and developing new leaders is constant work and needs to be a part of your mind-set.

Very few things will develop great leaders like the bus ministry. There are thousands of Christians across this land who have the potential to be great bus workers but have been overlooked by the carelessness of the pastor or bus director. Go on a campaign to find those people who, if given the chance, would love to do something for God. By the way, you will never find and develop leaders until you become the type of leader you should be.

- ◆ Leadership provides an avenue for service.
- ◆ Leadership provides training for service.
- ◆ Leadership provides encouragement in service.
- ◆ Leadership provides correction and instruction in service.
- ◆ Leadership provides reminders for service.

3. Check the excitement surrounding your bus ministry. Your church ought to be the most exciting place in town. The most exciting place in your church ought to be the bus ministry. How could you **not** be excited about it? Yet many churches have lost their energy and excitement. No matter how good a coach's game plan is, if he does not get the other coaches and players excited, it will not work. Get excited again, not just *about* the work but *in* the work. That is what leaders do.

- ◆ Write down your plans. A thought is not a plan until it has been put on paper.

◆ Promote those plans. Talk them up big.

◆ Communicate your plans. Meet with key workers to share your burden for souls through the bus ministry. Keep it in front of them consistently.

4. Develop determination with patience. Be determined that your bus ministry is going to do great things again and that you are going to see a harvest of souls as a result. Remember, however, that every harvest was preceded by much sowing and hard work. You must work with patience. Not everything will go as planned, but do not quit. Remember that "in due season" you will reap **if** *"ye faint not."* That is what patience is all about. It is not waiting for something to happen. It is waiting for the results of your determination and hard work to yield fruit.

5. Check your organization. Someone has said, "People don't plan to fail; they fail to plan." That is evident in a failing bus route or ministry. Neglect is the mother of disrepair. As I examine struggling bus ministries, one commonality is their lack of organization. Perhaps at one time they were organized, but with complacency has come neglect, and with neglect has come more complacency. Usually the lack or loss of organization is in one or more of three areas—facilities and equipment, workers, visitation. Here I briefly cover all three, but some will be covered in more detail in other chapters.

Facilities and Equipment. Some bus ministries need to upgrade their buses. I did not say buy new buses. Maybe you can get better buses, but at least make certain the ones you have look good and are mechanically sound. If your preparation has lagged, then I am certain your bus attendance has as well. We must be prepared and organized. This in itself provides a level of excitement for workers and riders. When the buses are cleaned, the classrooms are prepared, and the decorations are in place, these things provide a fun atmosphere for the work. It is important to your workers. It is important to your riders. It is important for your own attitude. On the contrary, it is discouraging to work hard to line up riders only to have a dirty bus or to have the bus break down.

Meet with your key workers and let them give you ideas that will help you be better prepared. Listen to them. They will be more enthused if they feel involved in the planning. Everyone will not have the same commitment, ability or talent; but everyone can contribute to the overall success of the bus ministry.

Workers. People don't fail because they want to fail. They fail because of a lack of leadership. Many times they fail because we have not done a good job of planning. They fall into the cracks of our carelessness. Perhaps a worker is not in a position suited to him. Perhaps he has not been instructed properly. People must know what their jobs and responsibilities are. They must know the location and times for their work. They need to have accountability. Someone has said, "You cannot expect what you do not inspect." There need to be paper trails that provide accountability. Keep records of things you deem to be important.

- hours visited
- contacts made
- problems that need further attention, like bus repairs
- people moving to another route
- number of workers that participated in the bus meeting
- number of workers on visitation

Organization begins with the leader writing the plans for workers on paper with enough details to make certain that every responsibility is covered. This should be provided for every job in the bus ministry, including drivers, captains, workers, teachers, etc.

Communication is a must. Bus meetings should be conducted on a regular basis. If not, we will have routes and captains conflicting rather than working together to generate success.

Our ministry is people, and people drive our ministry. A little organization goes a long way in making certain your people are ready for success and that you are ready for your people.

Visitation. This subject is covered in great detail in other chapters, but let me address it briefly here. If your bus ministry is struggling, it is probable that your visitation program is in a bit of disarray. Either you have abandoned the bus meeting, become lax in expecting all workers to attend, or you have failed to motivate and monitor the visitation of your workers. It may be all three. You need to fix this if you want to get the bus ministry on track.

◆ Revive it.

◆ Recommit to it.

◆ Rework it.

◆ Revitalize it.

6. **Plan a fall or spring program.** Many churches have drifted away from bus and Sunday school campaigns. I believe that is a monumental mistake. Study the chapters on conducting campaigns, and schedule one as soon as possible. The great bus ministries are the ones who have bus and Sunday school campaigns.

7. **Pray for your bus ministry.** When we pray, we get in touch with the heart of God. Have you ever noticed that prayer is usually followed by a burden and not the other way around? When you pray for your bus ministry, God will jump-start your heart with a renewed passion and vision. We must be in touch with Heaven and have the hand of God on our lives and work. Ask your workers to have special times of prayer personally as well as on their routes. Plan a special prayer meeting with all your workers and ask God to send a revival to your bus ministry.

8. **Start at least one new route.** Anytime there is a new route, there will also be new workers, more visitors, more people saved, more baptisms, and, as a result, fresh excitement. New birth is always exciting, so "birth" a new route and keep doing so throughout the year. If it is summertime, perhaps you could start a new route during Vacation Bible School. You could also ask all of your bus workers to cover a new area on one Saturday to help get a new route started. You could announce it in church and ask others to get involved in helping "birth" that new route.

9. **Keep the bus ministry before the people in your church.** Have testimonies about the bus ministry in your Sunday evening service. Allow bus captains, other workers and even bus riders to give testimonies of what God is doing on their routes or in their lives. Testimonies are a great blessing and provide a jump-start for a bus ministry by informing the entire church family of the good that is being done. Let them give testimonies about

◆ an answer to prayer,

◆ someone who was saved,

◆ a life that has been changed,

◆ a family who have been reached or helped,

◆ how the bus ministry has become a family ministry, or

◆ how the bus ministry has helped in teaching their children to serve the Lord.

10. Jump-start *your* **excitement.** Everything begins with leadership. Get that joyful spirit you once had about reaching children. If you are not excited, no one else will be. I stay excited about the bus ministry, and as a result we have an excited church.

Your bus ministry does not have to die, nor does it have to stay dead. Jump-start it. Bring it back to life and enjoy again the great blessings that accompany an exciting and vibrant bus ministry. By the way, don't wait until your bus ministry is on life support to implement these things. Use them to keep it going and growing all the time.

WAYS TO INCREASE YOUR
BUS ATTENDANCE

IT IS EASY to get into a slump on a bus route. Because we go through the same motions on Saturday and the same activities on Sunday, we begin to see the same old results week after week; or even worse, we begin to see our attendance drop. When attendance starts dropping, other things set in, like discouragement or dwindling worker participation. Eventually we lose our vision for the route. Without realizing it, we are in a giant rut; and if we are not careful, we will stay there or, worse, quit. It does not take much to get moving again. Here are a few things you can do to help you increase your bus attendance.

1. Work on your "want to"! You just "gotta" *want to* if you are going to get your bus route going and growing again. Make a decision in your heart and soul that you will not quit, you will not give up, and you will not allow the Devil to have the children on your route. Sometimes our thinking gets dull, and we fail to realize just what a difference we are making in their lives. Perhaps we forget the eternal difference we have made in those we have led to Christ, or we forget the importance of the truths and principles we are instilling in them. Maybe we merely lose sight of exactly why we are doing what we are doing and why we started in the first place. You need to remember that you may be their only hope. You need to decide to get back your "want to"!

2. Set a goal. A goal forces us to get back to the things we were doing when our route was growing. You don't have to set an attendance record, but set a goal to get your route going again. When we set a goal, it reminds us of the work and details required to reach that goal. Set a goal to increase growth by just ten over the next month and see if that doesn't help you get your route growing again.

3. **Spend time in prayer.** Sometimes we forget that we need God to keep the blessings flowing. Pray for God to give you back the burden you once had. Ask Him to help you see what you did when you first took that route—when you visited each house and person for the first time. Remember that broken heart you had? Remember the passion and desire you had for those children? Get alone with God and pray until God rekindles that fire in your heart.

4. **Enlist workers to help you.** Sometimes we just need some fresh excitement to help us push a little harder. Ask several people at church this week to help you next Saturday and Sunday to reach a goal on your route. I have found that when I take a new soul-winning partner with me, it motivates me in my witnessing or enlisting new riders. This encourages me to be a better example for others. A few new workers may be just the thing you need to get a few new riders.

5. **Prepare a good bus flier.** This actually could be a good idea to do every week. Maybe you are bored in preparing your fliers for visitation. That boredom will be felt with those who receive the flier. If you are not inspired by it, you can be sure that your workers and riders will not be either. Add some pizazz to your flier along with a new goal. Make sure that it will excite your workers and riders.

6. **Listen to sermons that will stir you for souls.** Sometimes our ministries quit growing because we personally quit growing. Once when I was driving home from a preaching engagement, I began listening to a sermon on soul winning and revival by Dr. John Rice. I had planned to drive halfway home that night and finish the 400-mile trip the next morning. Before I knew it, that sermon had so stirred and excited me that I had driven all the way home. There are many sermons that could stir you up about your bus route and soul winning. Get them and listen to them while you drive or work, and ask God to stir your heart again.

7. **Plan extra visitation time.** Saturday visitation is certainly

the best time to visit a bus route in preparation for a Sunday; but to get that route growing again, plan a Tuesday or Thursday evening time for some extra visitation. Make it your goal to win a bus family to Christ on that night. Extra work will often bring great rewards.

8. **Go to the parks or places where kids are playing and hand out fliers.** This will allow you to reach some whom you may not find just visiting door to door, and it could be the big boost you need to get your route growing again!

9. **Call your riders on Sunday mornings to get them up and ready for the bus.** This is always a good idea, but perhaps it is something you have forgotten or neglected to do. Make a list of the names and telephone numbers and call the kids about thirty to forty minutes before pickup time. This will allow them to get up and get ready before the bus arrives. With the use of cell phones, this is much easier to do than when we had only landlines.

10. **Reward not only riders but your workers as well for outstanding work on your route.** Often we spend money on promotions for the bus riders only, and that is fine. However, you may establish a reward or prize for the bus worker who produces the most new riders on your bus for a week or even over a month. Take him out to eat or to a baseball game or invite him to your house for a meal. Have him be recognized in church. No doubt your pastor would gladly recognize a worker that was responsible for bringing the most visitors to church.

Above all, do not allow your route to stagnate and die. It is far easier to build a growing route than to revive a dying one. Be conscious of the condition of your route and make certain you do all you can to keep it growing and reaching more souls for Christ.

A JUMP-START
IN SPRING

THE WINTER is finally easing its freezing grip. The ground is beginning to appear from underneath a blanket of snow or ice. A few buds are beginning to appear on the trees. We survived another winter, and in many places in the country that means we have survived some tough weekends on our bus routes and in our churches.

In much of the country and especially in our northern states, severe weather has an adverse effect on most churches, but perhaps nowhere is it more evident than in the bus ministry. When the weather is bad, many parents do not want to send their children off on a bus, and many children don't want to go out into the cold and blustery conditions. Sometimes the buses themselves don't want to cooperate in the subfreezing conditions. During the rough winters I am especially grateful for the faithful workers who get out on cold mornings and run their buses, not to mention their getting out on Saturdays and visiting their riders.

Southern states are often more affected because we are not as well prepared for the cold and ice. Here in Kentucky, cool weather has at times caused us to experience some tough weeks in the bus ministry. I know, those of you in the North probably laugh at us southerners who "get excited" over a couple of inches of snow; but we are just not as equipped to care for it as you are in the northern states. However, even northern bus ministries often suffer over the winter months, so spring is a good time to jump-start your bus routes. We want to do our best to get back our absentee riders as well as to attract new ones. Over the years we have found several ideas we use in order to do so.

1. Show appreciation to the faithful. Pastors and bus directors must never forget the sacrifice being made by those who work on your buses. There are weekends when most people avoid the elements, and the bus workers are out there doing their job **for no pay**—well, except for eternal rewards. In those winter weeks there are bus drivers, captains and workers who have faithfully loved and served their bus families every week in spite of the conditions. While there may have been some weeks that road conditions did not permit the buses to run, captains and workers have called, visited and loved those children who ride their buses. Without much fanfare or notice they have loved them, prayed for and with them, and kept on encouraging them to read their Bibles and do right.

The least we can do is to honor them and show them our appreciation. Someone has said that a "thank you!" is the greatest encouragement to motivate people to continue doing the right thing. We must make certain we recognize the efforts of our workers, but especially is that true when they have gone beyond what is easy or comfortable. Find ways to recognize your bus workers. By the way, Pastor, a personal word of thanks goes a long way as well.

2. Schedule a Round-Up Sunday. This is an old tried and true method of rounding up the strays. On cattle ranches the herd was allowed to wander out in the wilderness during the cold winter months in order to find shelter and food. In the spring the ranchers would mount their horses and head out to round up the strays. It was hard and often grueling work. There were some animals who had gone further out and others who had even gone through holes in fences. The ranchers did whatever it took to get them back. That must be our spirit in getting back those who may have strayed during the winter months.

The key to a Round-Up promotion is not usually the actual promotion but the excitement of it. Choose a promotion that the workers will be excited to promote. Food promotions always work well. For example, you may want to have McDonald's® Hamburger Sunday, Burrito Sunday, Pizza Sunday, etc. Perhaps you could have Mountain Dew® Sunday or Dr. Pepper® Day. Spring training for baseball could be an idea around which to build a promotion. You could have Spring Training Sunday and give baseball cards or other things that relate to baseball. Whatever you decide, plan a promotion that will excite the workers and that is a winner with the bus families. Here are a few other ideas.

◆ Kite Sunday

◆ Crazy Tennis Shoe Sunday

◆ Crazy Hat Day

◆ Silly Band Sunday

◆ Cowboy Sunday with workers dressed as cowboys and a cowboy hat given to all riders

3. **Prepare special fliers**. Design a flier that captures the excitement of your Round-Up Sunday. It needs to be more than just a black-and-white announcement. Make it exciting. Include the time of pickup and telephone numbers they can call for more information. Also include the name and address of the church, name of the bus captain or worker with cell number, and of course information about the big promotion itself. Study the way department stores, car dealerships and restaurants advertise. Don't let them be more excited about clothes, cars, food, and bargains than we are about the kids' riding the bus to Sunday school and church. Build excitement for your special day.

4. **Visit every family on your route**. Plan extra time to visit with every single family. Make sure every child in the family gets his own flier and maybe a few extra to give to friends he can invite to come with him. Perhaps you could give a prize to every person who brings a visitor. Spend time talking with the parents of each rider, rather than quickly visiting the kids wherever you may find them. Let the parents know you love their children and you appreciate their allowing their children to ride the bus to church. Make sure they know how big a deal it is.

5. **Spend at least one hour signing up new riders**. Nothing is more exciting than having new bus riders on a bus route. They

keep us sharp in our programs, prepared for our work, and focused on the Great Commission. Five visitors on your bus give you the potential for five young people to trust Christ as their Saviour. Get excited about that. Plan your day so that you have a section or streets where you will spend at least one hour looking for new riders. Make certain to see the parents in order to explain the program and the time schedule to them. Set a goal of how many visitors you want to ride your bus on the special-promotion Sunday, and get everyone involved in trying to reach that goal.

6. Spend one hour trying to win people to the Lord. There is no better way to cap off a day of bus visitation than to win someone to Christ. If you plan for it, pray for it and ask the Lord to help you, then you can do it. Perhaps you could visit a parent who needs to be saved or a teenager for whom you have been praying. God will bless your route because you are winning souls.

Make the spring a time of rounding up the strays in your ministry. Plan for it. Make it an annual part of your promotions. Precious lives and souls are at stake.

FALL ATTENDANCE CAMPAIGNS

THE LEAVES on the trees are turning colors, and the days are growing shorter. The kids are back in school, and the heat of summer has cooled into jacket weather. Like wintertime, summer is a time when many bus routes and Sunday school classes experience a bit of a decline. The distractions of summer can be difficult competitors for the attention of many. We can be angry about it, or we can accept it and do our best to reach new people for Christ and recapture the ones who drifted away.

"But when he saw the multitudes, he was moved with compassion on them, because they fainted, and were scattered abroad, as sheep having no shepherd.

"Then saith he unto his disciples, The harvest truly is plenteous, but the labourers are few;

"Pray ye therefore the Lord of the harvest, that he will send forth labourers into his harvest."—Matt. 9:36–38.

Fall can be an exciting time of year for bus ministries and Sunday schools. As we prepare for the fall harvest, we also prepare for the harvest of souls that can and should be reached for Christ. Some of our greatest growth through the years has taken place during our fall campaigns. Here are some things that are important in making certain the fall program is effective.

1. Schedule a time. I recommend a six-week period beginning in early October and going through the middle of November. September is a good time to begin promoting for your campaign, as school has started a new year and people are getting back into their routines. The first week of October is a great day to begin, and then end a week or two before Thanksgiving weekend.

2. Select a theme. You could build it around the fall theme or select something entirely different, but I suggest that there be some type of theme that runs through the entire six weeks. Preparation should begin far ahead of the scheduled dates, but let me cover some of the last-minute things you need to do in order to add a little more excitement and make the campaign a greater success. I recommend that you select a theme for your overall Sunday school and another for your bus ministry. That gives you two shots at building excitement in the people.

3. Communicate your plans to the leaders. Often the pastor, bus director or Sunday school superintendent excitedly plans an attendance campaign that he feels has great potential to reach many people, only to see it fizzle out and not fulfill its purpose or potential. That can usually be traced back to a lack of communication. It is important to speak of the plentiful harvest of souls that need to be reached and of your plans to reach them. That is exactly what Jesus did with His disciples, as we see in Matthew 9. Jesus pointed out the vast number of people who were "ripe unto harvest." Do not assume that others see the obvious potential that you see. Remind them. Point it out to them.

- ◆ Communicate your vision.
- ◆ Communicate your plans.
- ◆ Communicate your goals.
- ◆ Communicate your burden.
- ◆ Communicate your program.
- ◆ Communicate the organization.

4. Continue to communicate with your leaders and workers throughout the program. Programs can start with an explosion and end with a whimper simply because we assumed that everyone would stay motivated. Never assume that people will just stay excited without your encouragement. On a week-by-week basis, track your progress, recognize the achievers, encourage those that may have become discouraged, and instruct on how to keep striving. Have a weekly Sunday school teachers' meeting and a separate weekly bus workers' meeting. Lay leaders need this just as much as the church staff does.

5. The pastor or bus director should set the example in producing. It is important for the pastor to take the lead in winning people to Christ and in bringing visitors to church. We must lead by example. This allows us to share in the victories and blessings of a successful campaign and souls being saved. Many churches stop reaching their cities for Christ because the leadership stopped. People do what you do, not what you say. If you try to excite people to do what you yourself are not excited enough to do, your plans will fall flat.

6. Plan some exciting promotional Sundays. Having special days during the program is important. Here are a few ideas that may help you to boost your campaign to its end and even beyond.

◆ *Grandparents' Sunday.* This well-worn idea never gets "old" because grandparents are proud to be grandparents and children love to show off their grandparents. Have a time of recognition of all grandparents in church on this day. Honor the youngest, the oldest, the ones with the most grandchildren, the ones with the most grandchildren present in church that day, the ones who have been married the longest, etc. A potted plant is a good gift to present to each grandparent in attendance. Place a small sticker on the side of the pot with the name of the church on it, and ask them to pray for the children in your church each time they notice the flower. Encourage the families to stay and enjoy lunch together at the church after the service. Believe me, this is a great way to reach many people.

◆ *Harvest Sunday.* Young people love to get their very own pumpkins to decorate for fall, so you could give a pumpkin to every child present on this Sunday. You could even have a pumpkin decorating contest. The bus workers could judge the carved pumpkins when they are visiting the kids the next week and give out prizes the following morning on the bus for the top pumpkins.

◆ *No Absen__ee Sunday. Get it?* That was not a typo. Set a goal of having 100% attendance on your bus or in your Sunday school class that day. Prepare a roll of your riders and students, and set a goal not to have any Absen__ees. Then set a goal to have enough new riders or visitors to take the place of anyone who may be sick or out of town. If your bus or class reaches its goal, then have a special treat for each one in attendance. It is a good idea to have a treat prepared for everyone and an extra special treat if you reach that goal. No Absen__ee Sunday is always an exciting day!

◆ *Crazy Shoe Sunday.* This is a great and inexpensive promotion. On this Sunday everyone is to come dressed in a silly pair of shoes, and prizes should be given for those who wear the silliest shoes. They can be mixed, matched, crazy colors, funny shoestrings, etc. Bus workers should wear a pair of silly shoes when they go on bus visitation to let the riders know about the special day. This is a good promotion that works and adds a lot of excitement to the day.

◆ *Family Sunday on the Bus.* The goal on this is to get all of the people in the household to attend church either by driving in to church or riding on the bus. You will be amazed what this promotion will do. Ask a local restaurant for coupons to give to families that attend on Family Day.

Of course there are many other ideas, and I will be sharing more of these in this book and in future volumes. The important thing is to use your imagination and plan things that will attract people to attend your Sunday school and church. I recommend that some promotions be annual with some fresh ones thrown in as well. Some you might even decide to rotate. I have learned that people will look forward to some special days and even begin asking when the next one will be. That is a good sign that that particular idea is working. With the right work and planning, your attendance should "fall" forward, not backward.

A Few Good Ideas for Bus Promotions

THERE ARE many ideas for great promotions, and I could write an entire book just to teach these. Men ask me all the time for ideas that have worked for our church and bus ministry. When it comes to good ideas, I am not afraid both to borrow and to share them. I am not certain any of my ideas are original, but that matters little to me. My goal is to take what has worked for others and make it work for our church and then tell others about it. I never want to appear to take credit for any of these ideas. If I fail to give credit to someone who feels that one of these ideas is his, please accept my apology in advance.

My goal is very simple. It is to reach more boys and girls for Jesus through the bus ministry. Some promotional ideas may seem a bit too crazy, while others may motivate you. I recall once getting the idea for "Banana Sunday." I had a worker dress in a gorilla suit and took him visiting with me on my bus route. I just knew the kids would be all excited to see a "live" gorilla and it would give me an opportunity to tell them about the promotion on the bus the next day. It backfired. The little kids cried because he scared them. The big kids tried to be macho and fight him. I learned that day that some "good" ideas do not work out quite the way we think they will.

Nevertheless, the real secret to any promotion was what one of my mentors, Dr. Beebe, taught me. It is not the promotion that sells the excitement. It is the excitement that sells the promotion.

You have to get excited about something if you expect it to work. Here are a few ideas that we have found work well. When an idea works successfully, use it until it stops working.

Candy Cane Sunday. Encourage the kids to dress up like candy canes in red and white, preferably red and white stripes. The one who looks most like a candy cane receives a giant candy cane stick for his prize. All the others who dress up receive smaller candy canes. If a rider doesn't dress up, you still may want to give him a piece of peppermint candy. Encourage everyone to participate. Teach a lesson on the shepherd's cane. This is a great way to explain that Jesus is our Shepherd and we are the sheep.

Crazy Shoe Sunday. The idea for this day is for the riders to wear the craziest pair of shoes they can find or make. The craziest pair gets the grand prize, and everyone else gets a smaller prize just for participating. This is always a big success for our bus routes.

Grandparents' Sunday. On this day honor the grandparents who attend Sunday school and church. We bring the grandparents up to the platform and present each one with a gift such as a small plant. One Sunday I especially remember because we gave a begonia to every grandparent who attended. I brought all the grandparents to the platform to present to them their plants. It was then I first noticed the variety of these particular begonias. They were called Whiskey, Gin and Wine Begonias. Everyone had a good laugh, and I told them to smell them but not to eat them.

Chocolate Sunday. On this day every rider gets some type of chocolate candy like a Hershey's kiss. Those who bring a visitor get a Hershey's candy bar, and if they bring five or more visitors or if their parents visit, they receive a giant Hershey's chocolate candy bar.

"It's Still the Blood" Sunday. For this day we ask every bus worker to wear red clothes and encourage the children to wear red shirts. This is a great opportunity to teach them the importance of the blood of Jesus for salvation.

Picture Sunday. Set an attendance goal for each route and tell everyone that you will be taking a bus route picture that day. Display the pictures in the church foyer or lobby. Another idea is to send the pictures to the *Church Bus News* to be placed in our magazine. We will print the name of the church along with the bus captain and all the workers. Pictures are so inexpensive to reproduce that you can give every rider a copy of the picture the next week while out on visitation.

Bible Sunday. Emphasize bringing Bibles to Sunday school on this day. We teach this every Sunday, but occasionally it is good to emphasize it in a special way. There are several special things you can do for this day.

◆ Give a prize to everyone who brings a Bible.

◆ You can start a campaign lasting several weeks that encourages the riders to form a habit of bringing their Bibles to church. Give a prize to those who bring their Bibles every week of that campaign.

◆ Give an additional prize to those who memorize Bible verses that you assign them.

◆ Prizes for memorizing the Books of the Old and New Testaments are a good idea.

◆ You can give them gospel tracts and give a prize to those who distribute a certain number of them.

Fill the Bus Sunday. Use Luke 14:23, "Go out into the highways and hedges, and compel them to come in, that my house may be filled," as your theme. The goal is to fill the bus. Set a goal of 66 or 72 and involve the riders and their parents to please Jesus by filling the bus. This is one that was a great success for us when we used it as a big-day promotion one Sunday for every class and bus route. Everyone was excited to have a part in filling God's house.

Eating Out Sunday. Plan a nice candlelight dinner at your home. Invite the riders who bring the most visitors to come for dinner. You may have as many as five or ten who can win. Have them dress up in their best clothes, and let them enjoy a special evening or afternoon at your house. This will allow them to experience what a Christian home is like. It may also plant a seed in their minds and hearts to strive to have that when they are grown.

These days have worked for us, and I believe they will work for you as well.

Preparing for Successful
Attendance Campaigns

FOR MANY years I have successfully planned and carried out attendance campaigns in our church. These campaigns have effectively brought many people to Sunday school and church and even more importantly have resulted in many souls coming to Christ. I am a strong proponent of these types of campaigns. Those who criticize them have no idea of how effective they can be in attracting visitors as well as in encouraging members to bring friends and family members with them. My goal here is to lay the groundwork of what is required in planning and conducting successful campaigns.

These campaigns also allow us to get back someone who has fallen away, and many times such a one then remains faithful. I refuse to apologize for using campaigns to get people under the sound of the Gospel and the teaching of the Word of God. Some churches have drifted from the practice of campaigns, but there are many others that are successfully incorporating them into the programs of their churches. There are some things I have learned are helpful in planning and conducting such campaigns in your church.

I. Establish your goals.

A. The main goal should be to reach as many as possible with the Gospel. The bus ministry is still the greatest soul-winning tool in the New Testament church. It gives us the ability to reach the masses of people, but it does not replace personal soul winning, nor does it replace the work of building people through our Sunday school programs. However, we cannot forget the mandate we have to go out into the highways and hedges. We cannot overlook the command to reach those that will not be saved or come to church unless we go and get them. Set your goals to see a surge in the number of souls being saved. A campaign should be a time of great numbers coming to Christ, not just a time for increasing our attendance.

B. **Another goal is to reach families with the Gospel. Do not limit the campaign to children.** Don't overlook the parents and adults in the homes of the children who come on the bus route. While it may not be as easy to get them to church, it is certainly not impossible. It does take time and an investment in their lives. Often they are steeped in sin and cannot see their way out, or maybe they do not want to get out—yet. One of the keys to reaching parents is getting them to church and then getting them involved in an adult Sunday school class. They need a place where they can grow, meet other adults their age, and have a leader who takes an interest in their spiritual growth.

II. Be prepared.

A. **Set specific dates**. It is usually best to plan a six-week program. The best dates will vary from state to state. If you can avoid Sundays like those that fall during the spring break period, your campaign will be more effective. In Kentucky we avoid times when we are more likely to have snowstorms and/or ice storms, such as in February. However, be aware that people are anxious to get out when the winter weather begins to break. It is good to publish the dates early so your workers can plan their schedules and get their plans made for their bus routes.

B. **Choose a theme for the program.** The theme should be unique to each program. Choose a Bible verse or passage of Scripture as your theme for the campaign. This helps teach a spiritual truth or character trait throughout the program. Choose a theme that will excite the leadership of the ministry as well as the kids. Be creative. Make certain your theme is fun and exciting.

C. Set attendance goals. Have goals for each individual route as well as for the entire bus ministry. Have goals in a variety of areas:

- visitor goals
- rider goals
- family member goals
- salvation goals
- baptism goals

D. Select promotions. I recommend having a promotion for each Sunday. Again, be creative and make certain it will motivate people to do more. There are two types of promotions to consider:

- promotion for the individual bus riders
- awards given to bus routes, captains, workers, etc.

E. Decide on competition. There are various types of competition that can be utilized:

- Individual goal competition: For example, every route that reaches their goal wins.
- Teams competition: You can divide routes into teams and have them compete against one another.

F. Plan a big day. Either start your campaign with a big day or end it with one. Typically, we build up to the last Sunday of an attendance campaign for our big day. However, in recent years we have started our campaign with a big day instead. Both are effective and have their advantages. Having it at the beginning kicks off your campaign with a huge surge. Ending with it allows you to build up to it. Dr. Hyles would start his spring program with a big day and end his fall program with one. I have known pastors who had theirs right in the middle. In any case, schedule one big day during each campaign.

G. Promote the campaign. A program is only as good as the way you promote it. Promotion builds excitement, plus it shows that we have a plan for future growth. Even people who are not directly involved in the bus ministry can see that the ministry is productive and worthy of their financial support. Make certain you plan the promoting of your promotions as well as you do the actual promotion. McDonald's® may have a great promotional idea, but if they do not get out the word, it will not help them accomplish a thing.

◆ Promote well in advance.

◆ Promote from the pulpit.

◆ Promote on every bus.

◆ Promote the bus campaign in Sunday school.

◆ Have fliers for the bus riders to hand out each week.

◆ Have posters displayed in the church for everyone to see.

These are just a few ideas for a great attendance campaign. Get to work planning your next campaign; and remember that the more riders you have on the buses, the more opportunities you have to win people to Christ.

VISITING THE
BUS ROUTE

YOU CANNOT have an effective bus ministry without a faithful visitation program which has proper procedures in place. The next five chapters will cover various aspects of bus visitation. I will address this in five different ways, but you may find some overlapping thoughts. That is good because some duties of bus workers bear repeating because of their importance. Perhaps you have been a bus captain for many years and have visitation procedures you have followed a long time. I trust that these chapters will give you some ideas or reminders to make your visitation even more effective.

1. **Set aside a minimum of three to four hours to visit each week.** In most areas you may need to spend three hours just to visit all of your regular riders. Then, in order to maintain and grow your attendance, you need to visit for at least an hour to sign up new riders. I recommend that your main time of visitation be on Saturday because that way you are able to get riders lined up for the next day. Commit that time on a weekly basis and don't waiver.

2. **Go as a team.** I believe that it is good for all the workers on the route to go at the same time in order to make certain that your efforts are coordinated and that you maximize the time spent. This will build a good team spirit and allow you the opportunity to be prepared for the next morning.

3. **Have a definite time to start.** It is important to have regular bus meetings on Saturday morning. This provides not only

encouragement and instruction but also a definite time to visit on your bus route. When you visit at the same time each week, you build a relationship and testimony of faithfulness to the families on your route. I remember times when bus families had snacks or even lunch waiting for me when I came to visit. They just expected me to be at their houses at basically the same time every Saturday.

4. Have a definite time to finish. Do not just go with an open-ended quitting time. It is too easy to quit too soon or even to stay out too long. Working with a schedule is important in everything we do. A bus captain needs to be careful to get the workers back at the time he told them. Be considerate of your workers' time.

5. Visit throughout your scheduled time. Don't get into a habit of stopping early. Finish the job. It is easy to get tired or distracted. It can happen to anyone. We need to decide that we are not going to quit early. If things go more quickly visiting your regular riders, perhaps the Lord is making it possible to reach more new riders than usual. Don't take the chance of missing out on potential victories by quitting early.

6. Pray for the Holy Spirit to lead you. Often when we do something over and over again, we become dependent on self and experience. I wonder what we miss when we visit without asking the Holy Spirit to guide and direct us. Never visit without relying on the Holy Spirit to lead you. Pray as you go as well. Even as you are driving or walking down the street, ask the Holy Spirit to guide you to new young people whom you can invite to ride the bus.

7. Avoid time-wasting habits. Don't leave the bus meeting and go eat lunch or run an errand. This will diminish the effectiveness of the information and inspiration gained from the bus meeting. It also diverts us from the task at hand. It is important to go directly from the bus meeting to visiting the route. If you need a snack, pick something up and eat it on the go. Don't let anything deter you from getting busy visiting those kids. Do not let your cell phone distract you or your workers. In this Smartphone generation, it is easy to get into texting and out of the visitation mode. It might be a good idea to use your phone for emergencies only while visiting on your route.

8. Learn the names of your riders and their families. People love to hear someone use their names. One of the greatest compliments you can give someone is remembering his name. It means you have a sincere interest in him and that you care. Learning people's names will open doors for you to win people to Christ on your bus route. Try it when you visit this week. Use a person's name three or four times when you are talking to him. You will be amazed at how he will respond. This is true for adults as well, not just children.

9. Visit every rider. A weekly visit is an amazing way to build strong relationships with the people on your route. Spend a few minutes chatting with them. You don't have to talk about the bus ride until the end. You may want to use "Oh, by the way, we are having pizza on the bus tomorrow...." Whatever it is, you can mention it at the end of your chat. Make them feel you visit them because you care, not just to get them on the bus. Chatting for a few minutes each week allows you to know their spiritual needs so that you can pray with them as well as be a blessing to them.

10. Regularly visit those who have quit coming. You already know they are not coming, and you probably should not even try to get them to ride the bus. Stop by and just say hello. Ask how they are doing and let them know you are there for them if they need you. As you leave, say something like, "We would surely love to have you come to church with us soon. By the way, we are having ice cream sundaes tomorrow." Do not wait for an answer. Just letting them know you care can make an impression that possibly will bring them back in the future.

11. Learn the tools of being effective in your visitation. There are certain things you should always keep in mind and implement as you visit your bus route. Consider these:

♦ **Look for new riders.** Look for signs of children, like bicycles, toys, trampolines, and even lawns that are worn from children playing in them. Discipline yourself always to be on the lookout for new riders.

♦ **Be friendly to the children and families you visit.** They have burdens and need a captain that is always on the top side.

Show them that you are there to encourage and be a blessing to them.

◆ **Show an interest in people**. Be concerned for their physical as well as their spiritual needs. Jesus showed His concern for people by His attention to their needs. You should care about your bus children and their families. It has been said, "People do not care how much you know until they know how much you care." Caring goes a long way in winning their hearts.

◆ **Show excitement**. Nobody likes a grump. Your personality should be patterned after that of Jesus. He was always upbeat and positive.

◆ **Be aware of how you communicate with prospective bus riders and their families**. Read books that will help you to improve your communication skills.

◆ **Work to win parents and other family members of your bus children**.

◆ **Always have a flier prepared**. Even if there is no special promotion, fliers are important to stay connected.

◆ **Pray for each bus rider by name the night before you visit**. This will help you to keep a burden for your children and will increase your love for them.

It's Sunday morning and time to pick up the children who are waiting to ride the bus. This morning God will work in their lives through the program on the bus, the teaching in Sunday school, and the preaching of the Word in church. Souls will be saved, lives will be changed, and truths will be embedded into hearts. Never forget that this did not just happen. It is a result of the hard work of dedicated bus workers who took a portion of their Saturday and did what needed to be done on visitation. Commit yourself to doing this task in a way that can bring the most eternal results.

VISITATION CHECKLIST

E VERY effective bus route and bus ministry is built on many elements, not the least of which is a good visitation program. Any church that desires to have success in their bus ministry should be aware of the ways to make the time spent visiting most effective. In this chapter I am going to give you a simple checklist of things that need to be accomplished week in and week out to assure that you have successful and growing bus routes.

1. Attend the bus meeting. Bus meetings are important times for the bus ministry. I recommend that there be a set time on Saturday mornings when the bus workers meet together before going out on visitation. One important element of that meeting is to keep informed about information and instructions needed for that particular Sunday.

- ◆ You will need to get fliers for the coming Sunday.
- ◆ You will learn what the promotion is.
- ◆ You will know the schedule for the next day.
- ◆ You will find out about any changes that may have taken place for the next day.

The bus meeting is also a good time for encouragement, not only for yourself but for others as well. Hebrews 10:25 teaches us that assembling together brings encouragement. The bus ministry is hard work. These meetings are a wonderful way to be encouraged and motivated as you go out to reach the lost and visit your faithful riders. Your presence will not only be good for you but will encourage others who see you there.

2. Have a riders list with you. Every bus route should have a roster of those who ride that bus. It should include the names and addresses of

- regulars,
- occasional riders, and
- recent visitors.
- It should also have a place to add the names and addresses of new riders or prospects you find while on visitation.

3. Bus fliers should be ready and available ahead of the bus meeting. When everyone leaves the bus meeting to go out visiting, every worker should have an adequate supply of fliers to hand out as he visits. The flier should include the following information:

- date/day of promotion;
- promotional details;
- pickup time;
- church information—name, address, phone number;
- contact number—probably bus captain's cell phone number.

4. Have a visitation schedule. Make certain not to spend so much time in the meeting that it prevents the workers from finishing their visitation. Organize your workers into areas and then set aside time for visiting regulars and time for signing up new riders. Visit the entire length of time you set aside for visiting. Don't quit early. Be sure that you visit each person and family on your riders list. Saturday schedule should include:

- bus meeting
- visit regulars
- visit new riders or visitors from week before
- visit for new riders
- time for soul winning

5. Spend some time in prayer. Obviously, you want God to bless your efforts, and no matter how hard you work, you will not accomplish eternal results without the supernatural blessings that come from prayer.

- ◆ Pray for safety.
- ◆ Pray for souls to be saved.
- ◆ Pray for your workers.
- ◆ Pray for your leaders.
- ◆ Pray for the bus riders and their families.

6. Be sure that the bus is ready to go on Saturday. This is important because a prepared bus promotes good behavior and a positive atmosphere on the bus ride. Don't wait until Sunday morning. On the trip back to the church, everyone should pitch in and help clean the bus. I believe it is good for each bus to have a cleaning supply box with several items.

- ◆ garbage bags
- ◆ broom and dustpan
- ◆ window cleaner
- ◆ paper towels or rags

Incorporate these as a regular part of your visitation procedures, and your route will be ready every Sunday for a great day on the bus.

VISITATION INSTRUCTIONS
FOR BUS CAPTAINS

EVERY person who visits on a bus route is important to the success of the route, but there are some special things a captain should do to make the route a success. I have seen few successful bus routes that were not driven by the efforts of the captain. Take a few minutes and examine your efforts to make certain you are doing all the things a captain should do.

1. On occasion, the bus captain should visit all of the riders. While it is important to train workers to help in the visitation work, there is a special relationship between the riders and the captain. It is important for the captain to be the leader and to know the children and their needs. Just as it is acceptable for a pastor to be away from his church on occasions, a bus captain will have reasons to be away from his route from time to time. However, a church will not grow if the pastor is not faithful to preach to and lead the flock. The same is true for the captain of a bus route. You are the pastor of that route, and you need to make certain you know and lead those who ride your bus.

2. Learn to identify with each rider. Know their needs, their interests, their family, their likes, and their fears. This will help you to love them and lead them into a personal relationship with the Lord. If you do not have this quality in your visits, then your workers likewise probably will not.

3. Prospect for new riders every week. Even if you spend only a short time doing it, be sure that you sign up new riders every week. Be the example to your workers in this. Make it a habit. Teach it to others. Look for signs of children wherever you go, such as toys in the yard, playground equipment, bicycles, etc. Always have your radar up for signs of children in the area of your route.

4. Be extra friendly when you visit. Never forget the conditions in which many of our riders live. That should motivate you to be joyful and upbeat as you visit.

5. Don't waste time. Do not mix bus visitation with errands. It won't work. Do all of your visitation on a schedule and then set aside time to do your work around the house or to run errands. It is easy to get sidetracked if you try to do both at the same time.

6. Show your love and compassion for your riders. Assure them that the Lord loves them, the church loves them, and you love them. They need to feel your heart and know that you care about them. That is the purpose of the bus ministry and should be the heartbeat of the church.

7. Be enthusiastic, excited and energetic. I have met shy bus captains, but they were excited, shy bus captains. I have met introverted bus captains, but they were enthusiastic, introverted bus captains. The fact is that if you have a passion for something, you will be excited about that thing. The captain must show this when he is out visiting.

8. Be a good communicator. Know how to talk to people as you visit. A captain must be the best communicator on the route. Do not expect your workers to communicate your intentions and goals for you. You must be able to work with all the people on your route.

9. Do not argue with people. Occasionally people will want to argue "religion" with you. That is not your purpose. Stay focused reaching those you can for Christ.

10. Be brief. Learn to say a lot in a small amount of time. Do not appear to be in a rush, but keep in mind the many visits you need to make. Remember that more visits equals more riders. Use the time on the bus and the time visiting with a rider to build relationships, but be careful not to make visits too long.

When one of your workers visits with you, he should not be intimidated, but he should see all the qualities that a good bus worker should possess. He should feel you are good at what you do without thinking he could not do it. In other words, be the example of what you want him to be. You never know—you may be training a future bus captain.

VISITATION TO KEEP YOUR
ROUTE ALIVE

OCCASIONALLY someone will ask me what to do to revive his bus route. He is starting to decrease in attendance, and he wants to turn it around and get his route growing again. While there are many important things he needs to do, none is more important than making a few adjustments in his visitation.

It is crucial that your bus route continues to reach new people. A bus route not consistently having new riders is a dying route. Even taking just a break from visiting for a few weeks will kill a route. Getting new riders on the bus must be a regular weekly occurrence if you want to revive your route. Here are suggestions that will help you get your route growing again.

1. **Do not neglect weekly visitation.** You should be visiting all of your riders every week if you want them to attend consistently. When you don't set an example of consistency, you can't expect consistency from the riders. Sometimes we forget how long a time it is from Sunday to Sunday, especially to young children. To a child, a day can seem like a year. If you do not remind the riders every week that the bus is coming that Sunday, they might forget. You may be the only consistent person in those children's lives, so it's important not to let them down.

2. **Always take fliers promoting the following Sunday.** Little things make the difference between a struggling route and a thriving one. Thriving bus routes always have a flier to give out on

visitation. How long has it been since you took fliers weekly? In fact, if you are only using them for promotional Sundays or campaigns, you are hurting your route. This may seem like a small thing, but it is important to the success of your route. It gives you something to leave, then, in case the children aren't home. They will know you did not forget about them when they get home and a flier with a personal note is waiting for them. Get back to using fliers, and it will help your route.

3. Never pass up opportunities to reach new prospects. Many captains get into a rut and visit only their regulars. Ruts come from routines. While a routine is good, looking for new prospects should always be a part of the routine in your visitation. You are going to lose some riders along the way. A thriving route has new riders on a regular basis. Let me put it straight: sometimes we just get lazy. We take the easiest path and get complacent. Don't allow complacency on your route. There are children who will come if you simply invite them. You should always be looking for new prospects to ride your bus.

4. Involve your riders in inviting their friends. Thriving bus routes get their riders involved in finding new riders not just during programs but year round. Children will happily take you to their friends IF you ask them. To keep the route exciting, have special days that encourage the kids to bring their friends. Award a simple prize to the one who brings the most friends. Some of those friends will turn into regular riders, and that will keep your route growing.

5. Take someone with a fresh vision visiting with you. Maybe you are missing the signs of kids because you are too familiar with your area, and a new person may see things you do not see. Many times a captain will take the bus director with him, and the next day that route will have a nice group of visitors because the bus director saw what the captain was missing. Perhaps you could ask the captain of a thriving route to visit with you on a weeknight. Ask him to help you find new kids for your route. You may be surprised how many opportunities he will see that you pass by every week. Offer to do the same thing in return.

6. Go visiting on a weeknight. Shaking up the routine often helps shake off the complacency. You will be amazed at how many people are out and about during the week that you do not see on Saturday. New prospects may lead you to their friends and introduce a huge number of prospects for your bus.

7. Go door-to-door soul winning. Never stop knocking on doors winning souls to Christ. Decide to knock on five to ten doors every week on your route. That should only take about thirty minutes, but it will prove worthwhile. Some parents are more protective and will not allow their kids to play at the public park or down the street. Door-to-door soul winning will lead you to new prospects.

A struggling route may be the result of a loss of vision, or it may just be the result of a little laxity in your visitation. Take time to do an inventory of what you are doing in your visitation and make the adjustments needed to get you or even keep you on track.

TAKE BUS RIDERS VISITING
WITH YOU

ON ANY given Saturday morning on many of the routes at our church, a bus worker is out on his bus route visiting his riders. Right next to him is one of his bus kids. An exciting part of our bus ministry has always been the number of bus captains who take bus riders with them on Saturday visitation. This is often an untapped resource in some bus ministries. Some of our best bus workers were trained in this way. Obviously, you should make certain that you protect yourself and that you get permission from their parents, but you will see many benefits from involving them in your work.

1. **It allows the bus worker to spend more time with the riders.** This, in and of itself, is worth it. There is not enough time during the week to spend much one-on-one time with each bus kid. On an average, a bus kid spends two to four hours per week with his bus captain or attending a church service. There are too many hours in the week where the Devil can get a hold on his life. Saturday bus visitation is a good way to spend more time with them. It allows you to show your love for them personally. It doesn't take much to please a child and make him feel important. Most of the time he would prefer to spend time with you. Taking him visiting doubles the productivity of your time. You are accomplishing the purpose of visiting while investing time in the life of the young person.

2. **It is an effective way to disciple bus teenagers and teach**

them the importance of winning souls to Christ. Teenagers appreciate the time you spend with them, because many others often push them away. When you spend time with them, it allows you to teach them the importance of salvation, discipleship, standards, and other important truths about the Christian life. Teach them the importance of proper and modest apparel, and these will be the boys who ask for a shirt and tie or the girls who ask for a dress. These young people need an adult who believes in them enough to invest time personally in them, and they will respond to it.

3. **Bus kids can be your greatest help in winning people to Christ and getting them to church.** Most of us remember the first person we won to Christ and how exciting and fulfilling it was. Think of the joy and excitement that will run through your bus kids' hearts when they see their first soul saved. You will see it in the smile on their faces. They will work hard to get that convert to church so they can share with others that they won him to Christ. They will make sure others are awake and ready on Sunday morning. They will actively work at getting those new visitors on the bus. Every bus captain's desire is to see his love for souls passed on to others. What better way is there to accomplish this than taking the bus kids with you and letting them experience the joy?

4. **It shows them the way to live the Christian life.** Where else will they see the joy, the happiness, the work ethic, the schedule, and the love for the ministry if they do not see it in you? You are the only example most of them will ever have. They need to see the joy you have in serving Jesus as well as your sorrow for those who drift away. You are probably their only example of the Christian life.

5. **They will lead you to other children.** Teenage workers know where their peers live, and you would be amazed at the influence they have on others. Give them a chance, and you will see that they will be more productive than many adult workers. Let them catch a burden for the lost, and they will lead you to many precious souls.

6. **Let them help distribute extra fliers.** Taking them with

you will enable you to cover more new ground in a short period of time. It is easy for them to hand out fliers to other young people, and they won't ask for much in return. Just having your attention is usually enough. They just want to spend the time with you and know that you love and care for them.

7. It teaches them a sense of responsibility to others. Most children are told that they are not grown up enough to do anything important. Their parents may not even acknowledge their talents or gifts and may make them feel that they don't want to be disturbed by them. Allowing these young people to help you in the ministry will give them a sense of importance and value. Many of them are looking for something to which they can belong and someone who believes they have value. If you don't reach them now, other things will eventually be put ahead of God. The Lord has allowed us to have a small window of opportunity to work with these young people; and if we don't take advantage of it, that window will close.

8. It will please their parents to know they are doing something good and worthwhile. Most of the neighborhoods where we pick up young people are poor and a dead end for those who grow up there. Many parents lose hope in their children's futures. The world in which they live does not encourage or even allow them to think big. Seeing their children serve God allows parents to see the love of Christ through their children. I have seen some who were disobedient to their parents make a total change, and their parents were both astonished and thankful. Many parents are saved because of the change they see in the lives of their children.

An eight-year-old child rode a bus to church for the very first time. One of the first weeks he came to church, he got saved. Over the years he got involved working on the bus. As a young teenager he went visiting with his bus captain and eventually began visiting with the bus director for up to twelve hours on a Saturday. The highlight of the day was having lunch with the bus director. It gave him a sense of belonging. When he turned twenty, he got his Commercial Driver's License and drove the same bus he once rode as a child. By the time he was twenty-five, he had become the bus director in his church. He still remembers those days when someone came to his door and invited him to church, and he testifies to the fact that working on that route as a teenager had a large role in helping him to become who he is today.

Bus captain, bus director, pastor, do not take these young people for granted. This is the time to get them in the habit of serving the Lord. Their hearts are tender. They are ready, they are willing, and they are able. Take advantage of the moment while it is still available.

A Growing Route

W HEN YOU read that title, perhaps it brings thoughts of how to get more riders. There certainly isn't anything wrong with that. I often write about growing the numbers on our routes. Growth is always twofold—numeric and spiritual. Today I want to discuss the spiritual aspect of "growing your route."

My love for the bus ministry is deep. It comes with my love for Christ, for souls and for people's lives. The bus ministry is more than a way to increase attendance. It's also a way to see lives changed for Christ. What are some of the things a bus captain can do to help the riders on his route grow in the Lord?

1. Get them in the Bible. These children are saturated with the world's lies. We must get them in the Bible. Set up a Bible-reading program with accountability and incentives to get them to read their Bibles. We have a class for our teens where they receive a devotional book that guides them in daily Bible reading, etc. The bus route is a good place to set up programs for all the children to do the same.

Get the Bible in them. "Thy word have I hid in mine heart...." Why? "...that I might not sin against thee" (Ps. 119:11). Lead the riders on your bus to memorize God's Word. Use games and Scripture songs to get them actively learning the Bible. When we fill their minds and hearts with God's Word, it will not return void (Isa. 55:11).

2. Teach them to love God. The best way is to show them

how much God loves them. Paul said, "For the love of Christ constraineth us" (II Cor. 5:14). The more they know that God loves them, the more they will love Him. The Bible says, "We love him, because he first loved us" (I John 4:19).

Teach them to please the God they love. Love is not a feeling. Love is giving and pleasing the object. We teach them to show their love for God in the things they do to serve Him as well as the changes they make in their lives. We must be sure not to make them think they are earning God's love but that they are responding to His love.

3. Teach them that they have a purpose. We often lose kids to the world because they find their significance there. Help them to know that God had a plan for them before they were even born. Whoever values them the most will win them. We know that God placed the greatest value on their lives.

Help them find God's purpose for their lives. It is one thing to let them know they have a purpose, but we must show them how to find it. We can do this by not only praying *for* them but *with* them as well. Pray for God to lead them into His will. Call their names in prayer. For example, "Lord, I know You have a purpose/will for Johnny's life. Help Johnny to find and follow that purpose." You are not only speaking to the Lord, but you are leading Johnny to the Lord with your prayer.

4. Teach them Christian character. Christian character is changing the way we live, including our habits. These kids have often never seen how a Christian is to live. They have no idea how to behave. Get them around those who are examples of Christian character and then teach them how a Christian is to behave. A good coach teaches his players championship habits. A Christian leader must teach Christlike habits.

Help them live that Christian character. We must facilitate opportunities for these young people to put these things into action. For example, asking them to visit with us gives them the chance to dress the way they should, but we may have to provide the clothing they need. Applaud their actions. Let them know that God is pleased, and so are we, when their behavior glorifies Him. This is another reason why good behavior on the bus must be emphasized.

5. Pray with them. Jesus' disciples asked Him to teach them to pray because they saw Him pray. Pray about everything with your riders and talk about prayer. Let them know that God answers prayer. When you set a goal on your route, make certain prayer is included in reaching it. Let them see that God answered your prayers.

Teach them to pray. This is vital and includes two parts. The first is the need to, and the second is the "how to." When they come to you with a problem, always point them to prayer as a part of the solution. Inevitably they will want to learn how to pray, and you can teach them.

Bus captain, are you growing your route? As the numbers increase, are you also seeing growth in the lives of those God has allowed you to reach? May each of us do all we can to be active in helping to see lives changed.

For a complete list of available
books, please go to
swordofthelord.com.